M000206129

OUR
FAITHFUL
DEPARTED

"An important addition to the bookshelf of anyone involved in grief ministry in the Catholic Church. You will use it for support groups, reflections, homilies, and explaining how the Catholic tradition supports us as we grieve. I have already used some of the ideas Leonard DeLorenzo shares here."

Deacon Ed Shoener
Editor of *Responding to Suicide* and *When a Loved One Dies by Suicide*
President of the Association of Catholic Mental Health Ministers

"Leonard DeLorenzo once again invites us to take what we believe and hold it up to the light. In this book he gives us the chance to deeply consider what we think about the Communion of Saints, the dead, and eternity. Then he shows us how to apply the Church's teachings to our everyday experience and let them shape the way we live and the way we grieve. I want to give this book to everyone who is grieving."

Sarah Shutrop
Director of formation at Immaculate Heart Academy
West Milford, New Jersey

"For those grieving the loss of a loved one, Leonard DeLorenzo provides a loving framework by which to live in the hope of the perfect communion of we who live and the faithful who have died. Death is a universal reality of human existence and this book will help you learn how to remember, how to grieve, and ultimately how to love."

Dr. Kristin Collier
Director of the University of Michigan Medical School program on health, spirituality, and religion

"Thought provoking and Christ-centered. This powerful read is for all believers who search for soulful answers to life's biggest challenge—the loss of our precious loved ones. DeLorenzo bears witness to the truth: tending to the spiritual side of grieving is the surest path to hope, healing, and consolation."

M. Donna MacLeod
Author of the Seasons of Hope bereavement ministry series

Praise for the Engaging Catholicism series:

"The Engaging Catholicism series offers clear and engaging presentations of what we Catholics believe and how we practice our faith. These books are written by experts who know how to keep things accessible yet substantive, and there is nothing fluffy or light about them. The series is precisely what educators, pastoral leaders, and parents need to help hand on the faith, but these books should also be in the hands of anyone who simply wants to live their faith more deeply every day."

Katie Prejean McGrady
Award-winning author, project manager of Ave Explores, and host of The Katie McGrady Show

ENGAGING CATHOLICISM

OUR *FAITHFUL* DEPARTED

Where They Are and Why It Matters

Leonard J. DeLorenzo

McGrath Institute for Church Life | University of Notre Dame

AVE MARIA PRESS · AVE · Notre Dame, Indiana

Nihil Obstat: Reverend Monsignor Michael Heintz, PhD
Censor Librorum
Imprimatur: Most Reverend Kevin C. Rhoades, Bishop of Fort Wayne–South Bend
June 27, 2022

Unless noted otherwise, scripture quotations are from *Revised Standard Version of the Bible*, copyright © 1946, 1952, and 1971 National Council of the Churches of Christ in the United States of America. Used by permission. All rights reserved worldwide.

Translations of Second Vatican Council Documents *Lumen Gentium* and *Sacrosanctum Concilium* are taken from Austin Flannery, ed., in *Vatican Council II: Constitutions, Decrees, Declarations (Vatican Council II)*, Revised (Northport, New York: Costello Publishing Company, 1996).

Founded in 1865, Ave Maria Press is a ministry of the United States Province of Holy Cross.

www.avemariapress.com

Paperback: ISBN-13 978-1-64680-167-1

E-book: ISBN-13 978-1-64680-168-8

Cover image © iStock / GettyImagesPlus / maogg

Cover and text design by Samantha Watson.

Printed and bound in the United States of America.

Library of Congress Cataloging-in-Publication Data is available.

*To my father, who raised me.
And to his parents, who raised him.*

Master your feelings, listen to my words
and you shall learn just how my buried flesh
was meant to guide you in another way.
(Dante, *Purgatorio* XXXI.46–48)

CONTENTS

SERIES FOREWORD

Doctrine is probably not the first thing that comes to mind when we consider the pastoral work of the Church. We tend to presume that doctrine is abstract, of interest primarily to theologians and clergy whose vocation it is to contemplate lofty questions of belief. On the other hand, we tend to think the pastoral life of the Church is consumed primarily with practical questions: How do we pray? How do we pass on faith to the next generation? How do we form Christians to care about the hungry and thirsty? How might our parishes become spaces of lived discipleship? What are the best practices for the formation of Catholic families? Presenting at catechetical conferences in dioceses on a specific point of Catholic theology, faculty and staff of the McGrath Institute for Church Life often hear the question, "So, what's the significance? Give me the practical takeaways."

The separation between doctrine and practice is bad for theologians, pastoral leaders, and Christians looking to grow in holiness. It leads to theologians who no longer see their vocation as connected to the Church. Academic theologians speak a language that the enlightened alone possess. On occasion, they turn their attention to the ordinary beliefs and practices of the faithful, sometimes reacting with amusement or horror that one could be so primitive as to adore the Eucharist or leave flowers before Our Lady of Guadalupe. The proper arena for the theologian to exercise her craft is assumed to be the doctoral seminar, not the parish or the Catholic secondary school.

Likewise, pastoral strategy too often develops apart from the intellectual treasury of the Church. Such strategy is unreflective, not able to critically examine its own assumptions. For example, how we prepare adolescents for Confirmation is a theological and pastoral problem. Without the wisdom of sacramental doctrine, responding to this pastoral need becomes a matter of pragmatic conjecture, unfortunately leading to the variety of both implicit and often impoverished theologies of Confirmation that arose in the twentieth century. Pastoral strategy divorced from the doctrinal richness of the Church can leave catechesis deprived of anything worthwhile to pass on. If one is to be a youth minister, it is not enough to know best practices for accompanying teens through adolescence, since one can accompany someone even off a cliff. Pastoral leaders must also know a good deal about what Catholicism teaches to lead members of Christ's Body to the fullness of human happiness.

The Engaging Catholicism series invites you to see the intrinsic and intimate connection between doctrine and the pastoral life of the Church. Doctrines, after all, are the normative way of handing on the mysteries of our faith. Doctrines make us able to pick up a mystery, carry it around, and hand it to someone else. Doctrines, studied and understood, allow us to know we *are* handing on *this* mystery and not some substitute.

In order to properly hand on the mysteries of our faith, the pastoral leader has to *know a given doctrine contains a mystery*—has to have the doctrine opened up so that receiving it means encountering the mystery it carries. Only then can one be transformed by the doctrine. The problem with religious practice unformed or inadequately formed by doctrine is that it expects an easy and mostly continuous spiritual high, which cannot be sustained if one has sufficient grasp of one's own humanity.

We in the McGrath Institute for Church Life have confidence in Christian doctrines as saving truths, bearing mystery from the God who is love. We believe in the importance of these teachings for making us ever more human, and we believe in the urgent need to speak the Church's doctrines into, for, and with those who tend the pastoral life of the Church. We cannot think of any task more important than this. The books of this series represent our best efforts toward this crucial effort.

John C. Cavadini
Director of the McGrath Institute for Church Life
University of Notre Dame

INTRODUCTION: BETWEEN THE LIVING AND THE DEAD

I had just seen my grandfather a few weeks before his death. He was in the hospital, and in accordance with the directives of his living will, the feeding tubes had been removed. He was unable to speak and mostly unable to move, but it was clear he knew it when my brother and I walked in the room. I was the last one to leave his hospital room that night, staying behind to say goodbye and to whisper a prayer over him, tracing the Sign of the Cross on his forehead. It was the first time I had ever prayed with Louis DeLorenzo.

I had looked upon death with my grandfather once before, five years earlier. On a characteristically warm and wet Florida afternoon, I stood with my arm around my uncharacteristically vulnerable grandfather. The proudest and most stubborn man I have ever known was crying like a child in the rain. The woman who had been his wife for more than fifty years was lying in a cardboard coffin in the building behind us, awaiting cremation, and he had just kissed her forehead for the last time. Even at the end of a long and loving life, he felt her loss as an unmitigated tragedy. Dorothy DeLorenzo was gone.[1]

The tradition of *memento mori* tells each of us to "remember you must die." But that day in the rain, my grandfather confronted something else. It was not his own death that shocked and terrified him: it was his wife's. And five years later in that hospital room, as I traced the Sign of the Cross on my grandfather's forehead, I was confronting his death, not yet my own.

The death of loved ones is a real end. As a Christian, though, I am to believe that life is changed, not ended. My grandmother believed that. I am not sure my grandfather did, but I hope the same thing for both of them: that they live.

But how do they live? Where did they go? And what does this mean for us who remain?

WHAT THE PEOPLE SAY

Wherever the dead go, the overwhelming sense is that they are out of our reach. Since the mid-1950s, Gallup has been asking Americans about their belief in communicating with the dead. The question appears in different ways, yet no matter how it has been asked, only once, in 1998, did the number of people who answered affirmatively about being in relationship with the dead rise above 30 percent.[2] Year after year, for most people, the dead are silent and removed from the world of the living. The default assumption is that the dead are somewhere, but in no real way are they here or reachable from here. They have disappeared.[3]

When my grandfather was crying in the rain, it was the absence of his wife that he felt. Her body was there, but she was not. As far as I know, he never cried again in public, though my father would sometimes hear him sobbing alone in his room late at night. My grandfather longed for his wife's life, no longer present to him in her body.

When my grandfather died, life left his body, too. At his funeral, the well-intentioned minister assured us that Lou was now happily reunited with Dorothy and enjoying endless rounds of golf. His lifeless body was in the room, her lifeless body was in ashes, but those of us who remained were prompted to take consolation in a fuzzy image of them together.

That well-intentioned minister echoed the default assumptions of American religiosity: there is an afterlife, it is pleasant even if blurry, and it is removed from those of us who remain in this world of bodies. I realize now that in the more than 1,600 days between my grandmother's death and his own, my grandfather grasped something that the well-intentioned minister did not: it is the life in the bodies of our beloved dead that we miss. Dorothy's absence changed Lou's life, just as her presence did.

That is why I think the truly urgent question that no survey will ever be able to grasp is this: Do we live as though those who have died are in communion with us now?

That is a question about grief and mourning, hope and longing, memory and communication. It is also a question that Christians must address if we are to live what we say we believe.

TRANSLATING BELIEF FROM WORDS TO FLESH

What Christians profess is not always the same as what we believe. Of course, we profess the belief of the Church, but we only really believe in what we allow to take flesh in us. I can profess to believe in respecting my elders and treating everyone fairly, but I do not really believe in that if I habitually disparage the elderly and treat those less educated or less financially stable as my inferiors.

If I profess honesty but routinely cheat at poker, I do not really believe in honesty the way I say I do. (For the record, I am not good enough at poker to cheat at poker. Or am I?) Thus, we Christians must continually assess whether and to what degree we actually believe in what we profess.

By professing the Apostles' Creed at baptism, the Church hands on to us belief in the life that God nurtures in us throughout our Christian lives. In particular, the third part of the Creed is ordered to belief in the Holy Spirit, which unfolds into five specific and interrelated articles of faith. These are the ways in which the divine life, communicated to us beginning in baptism, grows in us toward completion in heavenly bliss, where God is all in all. The life given in the Spirit brings about

- the holy catholic church,
- the communion of saints,
- the forgiveness of sins,
- the resurrection of the body,
- and life everlasting.

Belief in "life everlasting" is not merely belief in something that begins once our breathing on this earth ceases; it is also belief in the everlasting significance of the lives we live now. In other words, who and what we are *now*—in this life—has everlasting consequences.[4] This explanation is likely to make us squeamish very quickly because it sounds a bit like judgment—as if we are held accountable for what we have done and what we have failed to do, for what we become and what we fail to become. But that is precisely what Christians profess to believe: that our lives matter because God makes them matter, and *other people's lives matter* because God makes them matter. Believing in life everlasting is not about valuing what comes after death at the expense of life in the world now; it is rather about valuing life in the world now—our own and others'—because God cherishes all life, now and evermore.

This emphasis on judgment and the eternal consequences of the quality of the lives we lead now might stir up notions of God as some kind of wicked Santa Claus: he's keeping a list, checking it twice, and most of us should worry about being naughty because our end won't be nice. But the life of the Holy Spirit is not just about securing the significance and everlasting meaning of lives lived in God; it is about the Holy Spirit healing our lives of the sins, fractures, and sorrows that lead to ruin. We believe in the "forgiveness of sins"—and this is balm to our troubled hearts, sinful creatures that we are.

Does that belief shape the lives of Christians today? We might be inclined to answer affirmatively, since most people hope and trust that their own sins have been forgiven or will be forgiven at the end of time. After all, only 0.5 percent of Americans believe they are going to hell, against nearly two-thirds who believe they are going to heaven.[5] But if we push beyond considering the forgiveness of sins as a gift for me and come to recognize it as also bound for others, we might think differently.

Everyone wants to be forgiven, but does everyone want to forgive? Believing in the forgiveness of sins entails committing ourselves to the painful and arduous work of forgiving others even now, seeking forgiveness from others even now, and trusting that this life of forgiveness will be complete in the heavenly kingdom. Belief in the Holy Spirit is belief that the command and power the Lord gives his disciples to forgive one another and seek forgiveness is the rule of eternal life from now on. The really challenging thing is the second part of that astounding petition Christians pray in the Lord's Prayer: "Forgive us our trespasses *as we forgive those who trespass against us.*"

To remain in unforgiveness or to fail to forgive others means remaining in a condition of fractured communion. The life of the Holy Spirit is the communion of the Father and Son, and the gift of this life for us draws us into that holy communion. The Holy Spirit makes us into one communion—the Communion of Saints. This is the true image of the holy catholic church: the one communion of those who share heavenly glory with those who still suffer under sin but seek that glory; the one communion of the living and the dead; the one communion that will be perfected at the end of time. This is the one communion Christ secures in himself, which he extends to his disciples through the Holy Spirit and offers to others through his disciples.

In the third part of the Creed, Christians profess belief in the Holy Spirit communicating to us divine life, which is a life of wholeness (see *Catechism of the Catholic Church*, 1). The Holy Spirit makes us whole in Christ. The dimensions of that wholeness are the holy catholic church, the Communion of Saints, the forgiveness of sins, the resurrection of the body, and life everlasting.

The Holy Spirit makes us members of Christ, joined to one another in him. We profess this, but do we live as if we are actually members of one another? And do we believe that we who live are still joined to those who have died?

PROCLAIMING THE DOCTRINE

At the Second Vatican Council, the Church's belief in the one communion between the living and the dead was loudly recounted and affirmed. In *Lumen Gentium* (the Dogmatic Constitution on the Church), the council fathers declared that "this sacred council accepts loyally the venerable faith of our ancestors in the living communion which exists between us and our sisters and brothers who are in the glory of heaven or who are yet being purified after their death" (51). When it came to the point of describing the one communion of the Church among her members presently abiding in differing stages of the pilgrimage toward wholeness in Christ, the council fathers went on to provide a comprehensive and compelling account:

> When the Lord will come in glory, and all his angels with him (see Mt 25:31), death will be no more and all things will be subject to him (see 1 Corinthians 15:26–27). But at the present time some of his disciples are pilgrims on earth, others have died and are being purified, while still others are in glory. . . . All, indeed, who are of Christ and who have his Spirit form one church and in Christ are joined together (Eph 4:16). So it is that the union of the wayfarers with the brothers and sisters who sleep in the peace of Christ is in *no way interrupted*; but on the contrary, according to the constant faith of the church, this union is reinforced by an exchange of spiritual goods. (*Lumen Gentium*, 49, emphasis added)

This passage provides doctrinal clarity on what the Church professes about the breadth of communion. It is like a commentary on the third part of the Apostles' Creed. Yet the council fathers proclaim near the end of the passage that the "union" between the living and the dead "is in no way interrupted." This small phrase would sting most Christians in the modern world—not to mention those who do not profess the Christian faith—as foreign, lacking in experiential support, and bordering on *un*believable.

What is death if not the interruption of the union between those who live and those who live no longer? The Church professes belief that, in Christ, the living and the dead are united, but when it comes to the practice of the faith—the belief that becomes flesh and blood—the overwhelming sense is one of separation.

My grandfather felt this acutely when his wife died. Then again, he was not a practicing Christian in any obvious sense. Does that mean that his sense of separation from his wife after her death—rather than union with her—was something that only non-Christians experience, including baptized Christians who are not practicing? Do "active" or "practicing" Christians experience more of a sense of union with their beloved dead than separation from them?

Just as "forgiveness of sins" and "life everlasting" are easier to profess than to fully believe, so "the Communion of Saints" as the one communion between the living and the dead rests easier on our lips than in our hearts. Though few Christians seem to understand how the "resurrection of the body" is integral to the Christian faith,[6] most Christians agree with and basically understand the other articles of faith in the third part of the creed.[7] While developing a better intellectual understanding of these aspects of the faith may be necessary and potentially healing in its own way, developing better knowledge is not the same as allowing belief to sink into your flesh and blood, reshaping your life in terms of what you desire, what you hope for, and what you treat as fundamentally true. You could *say* these things are true and yet not live as if they were true. The challenge to belief in this one communion is not a mere lack of understanding, as if it only required knowing the right things in the right way. The more challenging part is inhabiting the practices that slowly inscribe on the lives of the faithful what the Church proclaims from generation to generation. The words of Christian belief must become flesh. That, in brief, is the difference between what St. John Henry Newman calls "notional assent" and "real assent," as Timothy O'Malley helpfully describes in his book on the Real Presence that precedes this one in the Engaging Catholicism series.[8]

HOLDING ON BETWEEN MEMORY AND HOPE

The task of this book is to repropose and clarify the Christian doctrines regarding the communion between the living and the dead as proper to belief about the Church as the Communion of Saints. But a biblical and theological presentation of this belief will only take us so far, even though that work is important for guiding the faith of the faithful and proclaiming the Gospel. The movement from notional to real assent—from professed to lived belief—requires pastoral priorities and ritual practices. Those priorities and practices therefore also fall within the scope of this book. My hope is to help awaken the Christian imagination.

We have to imagine communion. Yet imagining communion is not just thinking about it; it is also picturing it, practicing it, and sacrificing for it. That is how the words of faith take on flesh and blood.

This book is not just for those who grieve their beloved dead. This book is for all the living, because none of us who live now will ever be fulfilled without sharing communion with all the dead in Christ. That communion is what we hope for as Christians, but it is also what we are commanded to practice. We do not truly live if we do not remember and love the dead.

I began my struggle toward this duty when I traced the Sign of the Cross on my dying grandfather's forehead as he lay motionless in his hospital room. For some time after his death, I struggled to find a memory of him on which I could build my hope for his resurrection to eternal life in Christ. I could profess belief that I hoped for this end for him, but allowing that belief to live in me was a struggle. I did not have the same struggle when it came to remembering and hoping for my grandmother: her faith had been apparent to me. Eventually, though, it was the faith of my grandmother that showed me how to hope for my grandfather, and it began with a particular memory.

For reasons I do not understand, what I usually remember first about my grandmother—in a vivid snapshot memory—is her sitting at the kitchen table in the slowly intensifying light of the early morning. The house is silent. One elbow is resting on the table, one hand pinching the skin above her brow, the other telling the beads of a rosary dangling near her knees. Her eyes are closed tight, and she has the look of intense, almost painful concentration on her face while her lips mutter prayers into the stillness of dawn.

I was only a child when I witnessed her thus at prayer, and I only saw her for a moment. She did not see me. But that memory is there for me all these decades later. I have no doubt she was praying for me, nor do I doubt that she was praying for her other grandchildren and her two children. And I am certain that she prayed morning after morning for her husband.

My grandfather's love for her and her love for him is a bond through which the grace and charity of our Lord may work. No one is saved alone. I have seen this truth illuminated in art, but to see and believe it in life requires an act of imagination and trust.

If you look to the lower left corner (from the viewer's perspective) of Michelangelo's *Last Judgment*, you will see those who are being gathered on Christ's right. The bones of the dead are coming up from their graves and their bodies are regaining flesh in their ascent toward Christ. Look closer and you will see that no one is rising alone. Those who are higher up are reaching down to pull up those still journeying to the fullness of life. Near the center of the work but still in the lower half—just to the left of the angels blowing their trumpets—there is one very fit and bright figure pulling up two shadowy figures. The figure in the light and the two in the shadows are not clasping hands; instead, each is holding on to something that looks like a rope. Look closer still and you see that this rope is beaded, like a rosary.

My grandmother prayed her rosary every morning. She prayed for my grandfather in life, I believe she prays for him in death, and I know that my call is to pray for him as she did, even as I pray for her and ask her to pray for me. I began responding to that call unawares when by instinct I traced the Sign of the Cross on my dying grandfather's forehead. The pressing question for me today is how to live as though he, who is dead, is in communion with me now.

That is a question not merely of doctrine but of practice: the struggle of living in communion with the dead.

1.

THE SEPARATION OF DEATH AND THE COMMUNION OF CHRIST

On June 18, 2020, Stephanie DePrez rushed into her family home. In the three hours since she had left the house, everything had changed. Her father was there, as he had been. Her brother was there, as he had been. Her mother's hospice bed was where it had been, with her mother's wounded, tumor-ridden body still pressing upon the mattress. But Susie DePrez was not there; Stephanie's mother was gone.

> I walked into the room . . . and there she is in her favorite shirt, and she's not there at all. I crawled in the bed and I held her, and it was a shell. She wasn't there. The thing that animated her—her soul—was no longer tied to this body. . . . I was holding her body—waxy skin, totally lifeless—and I just knew that she wasn't there. She's not here.[1]

Stephanie was touching her mother's absence. She knew her mother wasn't there because she tried to hold her and her mother

1

did not hold her back; she told her she loved her and her mother didn't say it back. Her mother's dead body was now a point of separation.

In this breath of time, what had been separated? As Stephanie felt quite viscerally, she had been separated from her mother. Her mother, who had been so present in that room not three hours earlier, was now separated from all who gathered there.

But Stephanie also felt another separation, related to the first. With her own hands she grasped that the life that had animated this body was now separated from it. Stephanie could not feel the life, only the lifeless body.

Stephanie knew that the lifeless body that remained was not her mother. She also knew that the life that had animated this body was not her mother. She had only known the *bodily life* of Susie DePrez as her mother. Stephanie wants to encounter her mother's body, but not just her body; she wants to feel her mother's soul, but not just her soul. Stephanie wants it all: she wants her mother—to feel her mother hug her, to feel her mother kiss her, to hear her mother say she loves her, and to know her mother as she has always known her: alive, bodily.

No matter how sophisticated our science and medicine become, we will never be able to give a better account of death than this: Death is separation. The lifeless body is the presence of absence. What ought to be, is not.

What happened? Words like "She died" are just placeholders, catchalls. When it is your loved one who is no longer present, the question of "What is death?" ceases to be merely philosophical. The question now concerns the source of your grief. What does Christianity say in response?

And what of the desire for reunion with the one who has died? The matter of "life after death" is in no way speculative when it is your loved one's life you desire after their death. This is now what you, personally, hope for. Your heart aches for a reunion you cannot even imagine. How does Christianity respond to this desire?

The questions proliferate: "What is death?" is tied up in the question of "What is the human being?" And that question hides questions about what the body is and what the soul is, which themselves lead to more questions: What does it mean for the body and soul to be in union, or to be separated? If you seek new life for your loved one, what exactly are you hoping for? Is it the same life they had or a different life, or does that miss the point? How could you be united with them? Is union possible now while you live, or only after you die, or not at all? (These are not questions anyone asks while grieving. In grief, we just bluntly encounter the seemingly inexplicable as pain and longing.)

Christians must ask Christ the crucial questions of what death is, what the human being is, and what it is we long for. He alone can show us the answers by showing us who he is and what he promises. We must seek the meaning of life and death in him who died and rose again, while remembering the pain of being separated from—and the longing to be united with—those we love. Our task in this chapter is to pay attention to the Passion, Death, and Resurrection of Christ. First, though, we have to learn the basics of biblical anthropology—of what a human being fundamentally is.

INTO THE DUST

Mary sinks into the dust beneath the Cross, the weight of her son's lifeless body pressing down upon her lap. I imagine her raising her eyes toward the city of Jerusalem, where all the people who drove her son out go about their day at a callous distance from her sorrow. The soldiers run through their motions, scoffing at this routine work. The friends who followed her son to this city have scattered, nowhere to be found. She alone holds her son, whom they killed.

No one else has known sorrow like this. There was never a time when Mary did not know him whom they killed as both her son and the life of the world. She held and guarded this mystery most tenderly, giving her own heart time and again to be pierced for love of him.

More than any other, Mary knows the depth of the offense. She knows that when they drove him out of the city, they were driving the Word of God out of human flesh. His body now upon her lap, she beholds his absence: the absence of God. She sits upon the dust, earth without water, clay without breath.

This is how God swallows up death: he succumbs to it. The mystery of Christian hope is secured here—and in what comes before and after. The one, undivided Son of God undergoes the separation of our death. *The undivided Son undergoes separation.* That is the last Sorrowful Mystery, and the first Glorious Mystery of our hope.

WHO DO YOU SAY THAT I AM?

The question of Jesus's identity is the primary question of the Gospel. Everything else points to and depends on who he is.

This question is not simply answered in various verses here and there; rather, each gospel is an answer to that question. In their distinct but harmonious ways, the gospels all testify and proclaim that this man is the Son of the Father. He is the Christ. He is the Word made flesh. He is our Lord and our God. This human being comes from God, goes to God, and is God, with us.

This is basic Christian stuff. But it is terribly difficult to hold to this fundamental confession when we see what becomes of Jesus. He appears weak in the face of power. He is vulnerable to betrayal. He suffers under the will of others. He dies. It is tempting to say or think, "That is the human part, not the divine part." But the testimony and proclamation remain unanimous among his witnesses: *this* is the Son of God—this man, Jesus.

One of the early church fathers, St. Irenaeus of Lyons, confronted teachers and preachers in his time who proposed alternative versions of the basic Christian stuff. After showing in his writings how all the gospels, one epistle after another, and every testimony of the Lord's chosen witnesses attest that the man Jesus was himself the Son of God, Irenaeus rebukes any who claim that the humanity of Jesus was some mere receptacle from which the Word of God was separable. That might sound like a silly theological squabble, but everything is at stake.

Did the Word of God *use* our humanity, or did this Word become *wedded* to our humanity? Was this union temporary or permanent? Was there an escape plan, or was God all in? It is easier to say that "Christ" drifted away from "Jesus" when the Passion began, or upon the Cross, or certainly by the moment of his death. It is easier to say that the lifeless body upon Mary's lap was *not* the Son of God, was *not* the Word Incarnate, was *not* the Christ. It is tempting to separate the "true Son" from this appearance.

Irenaeus, however, is conclusive: "The Gospel knew of no other son of man but him who was of Mary, who also suffered; and no Christ who flew away from Jesus before the passion; but him who was born it knew as Jesus Christ the Son of God, and that this same suffered and rose again."[2] Irenaeus refuses to excuse the Son of God from suffering the human condition because the Son of God did not excuse himself. "He passed through every stage of life," Irenaeus continues, and by doing so restores all to "communion with God."[3] The Son of God was not absent from what the man Jesus suffered: there are not two persons, but one Person who is the union of the human and the divine. "What he did appear, that he also was: God recapitulated the ancient formation of man."[4]

Difficult as it is to see, the dead body upon Mary's lap is the Son of God, the Word Incarnate, Jesus Christ. Mary holds the absence of absolute presence; this corpse is the point of separation of the inseparable God-man.

This is not a riddle; this is the heart of mystery at the fulcrum of sorrow and glory. As Irenaeus puts it, "God recapitulated the ancient formation of man" in this man, Jesus. The Son of God became what we are: the union of body and soul. And in his death, he endured what we suffer: the breakdown of that union.

This is the mystery we have to plumb: What does it mean for Jesus Christ, the permanent union of God and man, to undergo the utter disunion of human death?

THE CREATION OF THE HUMAN BEING

In the first two chapters of the book of Genesis, the creation of the human being is described three times, establishing the basis for what we may call a biblical anthropology. In our own day, as the meaning of a human being is obscured by technological incursions, gender ideologies, and a move toward individualization and "self-creation," a return to these fundamental claims is all the more important. When Irenaeus, writing in the second century, says that in Christ "God recapitulated the ancient formation of man," it is to this biblical anthropology that he is appealing.

THE IMAGE OF GOD

The first description of the creation of the human being comes on the sixth day of the first creation account in Genesis 1. God speaks these words to bring forth the last of his creatures:

> "Let us make man in our image, after our likeness; and let them have dominion over the fish of the sea, and over the birds of the air, and over the cattle, and over all the earth, and over every creeping thing that creeps upon the earth." So God created man in his own image, in the image of God he created him; male and female he created them. And God blessed them, and God said to them, "Be fruitful and multiply, and fill the earth and subdue it; and have dominion. . . ." (Gn 1:26–28)

In this first creation account, God is presented as both supreme monarch and priest, and obliquely as prophet. As monarch, God secures order and dispels chaos, not through any violent means but solely through the efficacious power of his Word: "God said . . ." (Gn 1:3, 6, 9, 11, 14, 20, 24, 26, 28, 29). As priest, God constructs a macrocosmic temple, with the sanctuary being the seventh day—the Sabbath—where his holy presence is all in all. Everything created in the six days of creation is directed to and intended for the fullness of worship on the seventh day. God blesses what he creates and calls his creation "good" (Gn 1:4, 10, 12, 18, 21–22, 25, 28, 31). As prophet, God separates things (light from darkness, water from land, birds from fish, animals from humans, etc.) and speaks them into their proper places. When God creates human beings in his image, then, he creates them to do as he does: to give order and dispel chaos; to direct all things to worship of God and offer blessings; and to separate things into their proper places. Human beings must thus become cocreators (or subcreators), exercising our creativity and reason to draw all things toward God's wisdom and glory. That exercise of freedom and agency is the "dominion" Genesis 1:26 and 1:28 name. God exercises absolute dominion and creates human beings to exercise dominion after his pattern.

The "image of God" is stressed twice in verse 1:27, which describes the creation of human beings as "male and female," the two distinct ways of being a human being. With the assistance of later Christian trinitarian theology, we come to understand God as "three Persons, one God": the Father and Son are distinct, yet in eternal communion: the Holy Spirit. Communion means not sameness but the union of distinct Persons. This communion amid distinction is the image of God in which human beings are created and essential to what it means to be a human being. The basic distinction among human beings is between male and female, and their union—principally in marriage—manifests God's image.

From the Genesis 1 creation account, we discern that the human being is created in God's image in four ways. After God's kingly character, human beings are created and called upon to bring order and govern wisely. After God's priestly character, human beings are created and called upon to orient all things toward worship and offer blessings. After God's prophetic character, human beings are created and called upon to separate into their proper places what is otherwise confused. And after God's triunity, human beings are created distinctly for the sake of communion.

By the Incarnation, when the Word of God comes to dwell in human flesh, God enters into union with what he created in his image, after his own likeness.

THE UNION OF BODY AND SOUL

The second description of the creation of the human being occurs at the outset of the creation account in Genesis 2. In this account, God is the LORD God, which is a more personal name and indicative of his intimate relations with human beings. (By the way, the serpent changes the LORD God's name when he first speaks to the woman, which shows that sin begins, in part, by making God impersonal—see Genesis 3:1–3.) The LORD God is a potter, who shapes his creature with his own hands. The LORD God is the intimate life-giver, who donates his own breath to his creature. We hear of the creation of the first human being in this manner:

"The LORD God formed man from the dust of the earth. He blew into his nostrils the breath of life, and man became a living being" (Gn 2:7, JPS).

On the basis of this single but crucial verse, we may say that the human being is intentionally formed "earth stuff" that is given breath. The formed earth stuff alone is not a human being, nor is the given breath alone a human being. The human being lives only through the union of these two. The human being is in fact a living union.

The verse in translation conceals one very important detail regarding the formation of "man." Were we reading this in Hebrew we would see that the word translated here as "man" would be *'adam*, while the word "earth" would be *'adamah*. *'Adam* is not yet a proper name but rather a word of relation: *'adam* is the one who is from the *'adamah*. To capture this more literally in English, we might say that the "earth creature" is intentionally formed from the "earth." Thus the "man" whom the LORD God forms is created in harmony with the earth from the beginning.

When we look upon the breath of life given directly from the LORD God to his creature, there is not something hidden in translation here but instead something we ought to pause to consider more fully. This is the most intimate act imaginable. This Creator gives his own breath for his creature to breathe as his own. We see here the deep harmony between the human being and the LORD God.

The union of intentionally formed earth stuff and the breath intimately given is what makes man "a living being." It is not difficult to think of the intentionally formed earth stuff as the body and the breath intimately given as the soul, so that the second creation account begins with the description of the human being as the living union of body and soul. Over and over again, St. Irenaeus will speak of the human being as "the whole man," by which he means not just the body, not just the soul, but indeed the union of the body and soul. The body and soul are created in harmony, and by their union there is a living human being.[5]

By the Incarnation, when the Word of God comes to dwell in human flesh, God unites himself not just to body and not just to soul but indeed to his creature who is the union of body and soul.[6]

ONE FLESH

The third and final description of the creation of the human being in the opening chapters of Genesis occurs at the end of the second creation account. Having found no suitable partner for the "man"—'adam—in all creation, the LORD God creates a suitable partner so that the man will not be alone, because, as the LORD God says, being alone "is not good" (Gn 2:18).

> So the LORD God caused a deep sleep to fall upon the man, and while he slept took one of his ribs and closed up its place with flesh; and the rib which the LORD God had taken from the man he made into a woman and brought her to the man. Then the man said,
>> "This at last is bone of my bones
>>> and flesh of my flesh;
>> she shall be called Woman ['ishshah],
>>> because she was taken out of Man ['ish]."

Therefore a man leaves his father and his mother and
clings to his wife, and they become one flesh. (Gn
2:21–24)

In completing the second creation account, this act of creation reveals to us that the human being who is the living union of body and soul is not complete alone. Just as in the first creation account, when God created human beings in his image as male and female—distinct and ordered to communion—so here the human being is only complete in communion. The two human beings are not identical; they are distinct. And yet it is precisely as distinct that they "cling" to each other and become "one flesh." The communion Man and Woman forge does not yield sameness, nor does it indicate absorption of one into the other. The two do not have the same name; in fact, each receives a new name in light of the other: Man and Woman (Gn 2:23), or *'ish* and *'ishshah*, which are names of relation, like "husband" and "wife" in English. Although both are created directly by the LORD God and both are the living union of body and soul, they are not the same creature. Being alone was "not good," because what is good is being in communion. Human beings are only truly themselves in communion.

By the Incarnation, when the Word of God comes to dwell in human flesh, God clings to what is utterly distinct from him—creatureliness—and reveals the union of love on which the communion of human beings is based.

BIBLICAL ANTHROPOLOGY AND DEATH

These testimonies about the creation of the human being are at least as revelatory of who God is as they are of what it means to be human. In Genesis 1:26–28, God creates human beings in his own image—in other words, to resemble him. We are not the same as God, but who and what we are is analogous to who and what God is. Not only by calling us to exercise dominion but also by creating us in communion and for communion, God's "ancient formation of man" is according to the divine image.

In Genesis 2:7, the LORD God creates the human being as the union of body and soul. To forge this union, the LORD God directly and intimately labors over his creature. The body of the human being is the work of the LORD God, even as it is formed from the stuff of creation. The soul of the human being is the living breath of the LORD God, which the Creator gives his creature. And the union between the body and the soul is the seal of the LORD God's craftsmanship, so that the stuff of earth and the breath of heaven are bound together in this unique creature of God: the human being.

In Genesis 2:21–24, the LORD God again makes communion the original condition and final orientation of human beings. The LORD God creates human beings so that we are not complete in ourselves, but only in communion. The LORD God builds toward communion in all his works.

What does this biblical anthropology mean for a daughter holding the lifeless body of her mother? It says that what she touches should not be.

- In death, we lose dominion: the creative power to order and ordain is stripped from us.
- In death, we lose the union of body and soul: the bond that makes the human being what she is, is broken.
- In death, we lose communion: those who have come to cling to one another in love are separated from one another.

This is the meaning of *human* death. And it was a human death that the Only Begotten Son of God endured in becoming fully human.

THE PASCHAL MYSTERY

"Truly this man was the Son of God" (Mk 15:39; Mt 27:54; cf. Lk 23:47). These are the first words anyone speaks immediately after the death of Jesus in both the Gospel of Mark and the Gospel of Matthew. The proclamation comes from the most unlikely person: a Roman centurion overseeing the execution. What he has just witnessed is certainly something he has witnessed numerous times before: the death of a man. But in gazing upon this dead man, he proclaims Jesus's true identity.

Like every human death, the death of Jesus entails the loss of dominion, the loss of the union of body and soul, and the loss of communion. But in this case, it is truly the Son of God who undergoes this loss. The centurion bears witness to a mystery he does not understand. Death, it seems, has been given power over the Word of Life.

This death did not happen in a moment. We can look back earlier to see how Jesus was deliberately entering into death. He did not will his own death, but he did will to share in the condition of those of us who suffer death. We could follow him all the way back to the beginning, though even by moving back to the night before the centurion's proclamation we can see how Jesus most assuredly enters into the conditions of human death. We must continually remember that it is the Son of God who is doing this.

Confessing Jesus as the Son of God means that we do not have any power over him. He is free of our control—unless he chooses to put himself under our control. "You would have no power over me," Jesus says to Pilate, "unless it had been given you from above" (Jn 19:11). This truth is absolutely crucial for us in tracing Jesus's path to his Crucifixion and burial. What he undergoes is the result of what God has freely chosen, before any of this concerns the action of man. Echoing the entire Christian tradition around whether God can suffer, the twentieth-century Catholic theologian Hans Urs von Balthasar writes, "There can be no *pathos* [suffering] in God if by this we mean some involuntary influence from the outside. . . . God (and this applies to the Incarnate One also) can only be 'passive,' . . . if this accords with some prior, 'active,' free decision."[7] This is a commentary on what Jesus says to Pilate: What you do to me is preceded by what has been divinely willed, which is that I should enter into this death.

St. Paul, in his Letter to the Philippians, contemplates this same mystery in his great hymn to the Incarnation and Passion of the Son of God: "Christ Jesus, . . . though he was in the form of God, did not count equality with God a thing to be grasped, but emptied himself, taking the form of a servant, being born in the likeness of men. And being found in human form he humbled himself and became obedient unto death, even death on a cross" (Phil 2:5–8). The Son of God, in obedience to his Father's will, elects to be in solidarity with us poor sinners even to the extent of sharing in what we suffer in death because of sin: the loss of communion, the loss of dominion, and even the loss of the union of our bodies and souls. "Truly this was the Son of God," who humbles himself to share in our inglorious end so as to give us in himself a glorious new beginning.

In that exchange, Christian hope is born.

From the Last Supper to Gethsemane: Communion and Its Undoing

On the night before he dies, Jesus gathers his twelve apostles in an upper room. Taking the unleavened bread of Passover, he blesses and breaks this bread, and gives it to his apostles as his own Body. He becomes their Passover sacrifice. When supper ends, he takes the cup of wine and blesses it, gives it to them, and says that this, his Blood, is the blood of the new covenant. Here, gathered around this sacrificial offering, are the twelve apostles as the figures of the twelve tribes of Israel. Here, gathered together, are his friends and companions, his disciples whom he chose out of his prayer. Here, he is the vine, and they are his branches. Here is the source and summit of communion.

No sooner has this sacrificial offering been made than one of the Twelve who shared in this communion goes out to orchestrate Jesus's arrest. And immediately the rest of the apostles begin arguing about which of them will be the greatest (see Luke 22:24–27). Here, at the heart of communion, the bonds of love begin to break.

From the upper room, Jesus leads his disciples out to the mount called Olivet, toward a garden called Gethsemane. Judas Iscariot no longer with them, he instructs eight of his disciples to stay in a certain place while he goes up farther to pray. He takes his three most intimate disciples with him: Peter, James, and John. To them, he says "My soul is very sorrowful, even to death; remain here, and watch" (Mt 26:38; Mk 14:34; cf. Lk 22:40). And then he goes on a little farther to pray. There are now three levels on Olivet: at the base are the eight disciples, who ought to pray; farther up are the three intimate disciples, who ought to keep watch and share in Jesus's sorrow; and at the peak is Jesus, who prays in agony. He ought not be alone, for his disciples should exercise communion with him through their prayer and by sharing in his sorrow, but as we soon see, their prayer with him and their will to share his sorrow are weak. He will be taken alone.

"My Father, if it be possible, let this chalice pass from me; nevertheless, not as I will, but as thou wilt" (Mt 26:39). For the chalice to pass, the hearts of his persecutors would have to be changed, but his Father will not change their hearts by force, nor does Jesus ask for that. For the chalice to pass, his apostles would have to cling to him, refusing to let him suffer alone, but his Father will not force them to love his Son with all they have, and Jesus does not ask for that either. In everything that follows, Jesus will entrust himself to his Father as he has throughout his life. But now, as he gives himself to his Father, each of the apostles who have been dear to him will break away, with only the beloved disciple returning to receive Jesus's mother as he hangs upon the Cross.

The Son's obedience to his Father means absorbing the cost of betrayal, experiencing the pain and deep sadness of abandonment. At the very moment he offers the fullness of communion in the upper room, those who receive his gift begin to deny him. He becomes a vine without his branches. His death will consummate the movement of his apostles to separate from him.

By giving them his Body and his Blood, Jesus puts himself into the hands of his disciples. He lets them decide their bond with him through his Passion.

Into the Households of Power: The Reversal of Dominion

The nighttime arrest of Jesus initiates an absurd parade of posturing. A band of soldiers follows Judas to the place where Jesus was known to pray. They come bearing arms, in a show of might. These are not the terms of Jesus's power—he bears no arms. He gives himself into their hands.

Throughout the night and into the next day, Jesus is taken from one hall of power to another. First, he is taken to the household of the former high priest Annas, who presumes authority over Jesus (see John 18:13). Next, Jesus is taken to Annas's son-in-law, Caiaphas, who is currently serving as high priest and who is no doubt trying to step out from Annas's shadow to be his own man. From Annas and Caiaphas, Jesus is taken to the Roman prefect Pontius Pilate. The religious authorities have claimed power over Jesus, and now imperial authority will have its turn. Pilate is bored by this provincial matter and, seeking to be done with it, sends Jesus to Herod, the tetrarch of Jesus's home province of Galilee, who is visiting Jerusalem for Passover (see Luke 23:8–12). Herod fancied himself a regal figure of importance, and with Jesus in his custody, he and his soldiers "treated him with contempt and mocked him; then, clothing him in gorgeous apparel, . . . sent him back to Pilate" (Lk 23:11).

All through the night and into the next day, Jesus is paraded through these chambers of power where arrogance and callousness make a mockery of his true identity

- Annas and Caiaphas make a mockery of Jesus's priestly identity. Presuming to possess the power to bless and to curse, they curse the Son of God in the name of God.
- Herod makes a mockery of Jesus's kingly identity. Resorting to satirical means to secure the order he himself prefers, he ridicules the King of the Jews with a king's pride.
- Pilate makes a mockery of Jesus's prophetic identity. Casual in his regard for the truth, he moves matters along with bureaucratic indifference and passes judgment on the Truth.

By refusing to dignify the might of those who presume power, Jesus allows this parody of dominion to play out at his expense. He lets them take his power.

Atop Calvary: The Release of Union

By late morning, upon the final verdict from Pilate, the soldiers press wooden beams upon Jesus's shoulders. The people who acclaimed his arrival in Jerusalem five days earlier now drive him out. He is sleep deprived, filled with sorrow, and alone. Having been scourged, his body is weak. Three times he collapses under the weight of it all. His control over his own body is failing as the jeering that surrounds him crescendos. His heart is broken.

Outside the gates and atop the chosen mount, Jesus is nailed to the Cross and lifted up above the trailing crowd. He is suspended between his Father above and the people below. From up here, he looks downward. He sees his own body. He gazes upon this marvel of creation—the human body, this wondrous instrument. And at the same time he sees upon this body—his body—the indignities heaped upon it. He loves his body. He grieves over his body:

> A body you have prepared for me. . . . Behold, I come to do your will, O God (Heb 10:5, 7; cf. Ps 40:6–8).

> For you formed my inmost parts, you knitted me together in my mother's womb. I praise you, for I am wondrously made! (Ps 139:13–14).

Below he sees his mother, in whom and from whom he became flesh. He hangs as the living body that came from her. This is the body she nurtured and cared for. He is her son.

> Then Jesus, crying with a loud voice, said, "Father, into your hands I commit my spirit!" And having said this he breathed his last (Lk 23:46).

> And Jesus uttered a loud cry, and breathed his last (Mk 15:37).

> And Jesus cried again with a loud voice and yielded up his spirit (Mt 27:50).

> "It is finished"; and he bowed his head and gave up his spirit (Jn 19:30)

Jesus entrusts himself in the end to his Father. He gives everything, including his death, over to the Father, from whom he has received everything. And what remains is his lifeless body, which is placed upon Mary's lap.

By refusing to force anyone to love him, Jesus allows the people to drive their God out of their midst, even to the point of seeming to separate the divine life from the human flesh of the Incarnation's union. He lets the disunion of death happen to him.[8] And there—right there—is his mother, clinging to his body, feeling the absence of him whom she loves.

In the Darkness of the Tomb: The Final Descent

Where has the Son of God gone? Mary knows her son is dead. The centurion knows this man is dead. Those near the Cross heard him commit his spirit to his Father and then saw him die. Where has he gone?

His body is taken to a tomb and prepared for burial. His body is laid out upon rock, and a stone is rolled over the entrance to the tomb. Everybody leaves and his body remains in the darkness of the tomb. Where is the Son of God?

No one sees and no one hears, but in faith the Church discerns where the Son of God has gone. The body lying in the tomb, the spirit handed over: this is the Son of God. He is never divided, and now he holds within himself the utter separation of the body and the soul of human death. The one Son of God abides in this separation. The two are made one in him, and what God has joined in himself no man can sunder.

In an ancient homily for Holy Saturday, the mystery of this dark and silent time following the death of Jesus is made into a hymn of the union that is hereby being forged. What was broken apart is being brought together in him; what was lost is being found. "God has died in the flesh," the hymn proclaims, "and the underworld has trembled."[9] The Lord himself goes to where Adam, the first man, lies waiting. In going to the first man, who fell in sin, the LORD goes to gather all the dead: "I am your God, who for your sake became your son, who for you and your descendants now speak and command with authority those in prison: Come forth, and those in darkness: Have light, and those who sleep: Rise."[10]

Among the dead, Christ speaks with authority, because he is the one through whom all things were created (see John 1:3; Colossians 1:16). They who were created have collapsed, but his authority is unchecked. This man is no mere man. He is the Son of God; his dominion is absolute.

The Son of God has taken on the condition of those who have forfeited their dominion, who have lost communion with the living, whose living union of body and soul has been broken. By this ancient homily we hear how Christ shares in the condition of the dead so that, through this solidarity, they may come to share in what he himself is. He is the Son of the Father. He is the Word of Life. He is the communion of the living and the dead. "Arise, O man, work of my hands, arise, you who were fashioned in my image. Rise, let us go hence; for you in me and I in you, together we are one undivided person."[11]

When the Word of God joined with human flesh, he became the new principle of the union of the human person. He is one undivided person, and he chose those he loves to be in union with him. This is what was intended from the beginning: "And they become one flesh" (Gn 2:24).

"Look at the spittle on my face, which I receive because of you, in order to restore you to that first divine inbreathing at creation. See the blows on my cheeks, which I accepted in order to refashion your distorted form to my own image."[12] The Passion that Christ endured was the work of a new creation. While others spit upon his face, he was preparing to animate dead flesh with his divine life. While they marred his body with cruelty, he was preparing his body as the source of forgiveness. The fashioning of a body and the gift of breath are the terms of the creation of *'adam* in Genesis 2:7, but now the living union of body and soul is the union of God and creation in Jesus, the Son: "Now I myself am united to you, I who am life."[13]

This is ground zero of Christian hope, Christian hope starting from the absolute bottom. His body lying lifeless for a day in the darkness of the tomb, his spirit given in obedience to the Father, the Son of God shares with all the dead in the loss of dominion, the loss of communion, and the loss of union. But in this lifeless state, the dominion of God becomes supreme, now dawning upon the dead. The solidarity of the Son of God with the lonely dead becomes the new and everlasting communion. His life becomes the new union for their bodies and souls, so that when they rise, they will rise like him: fully human.[14]

St. Irenaeus concludes that "nothing is so ignoble as dead flesh, and nothing so glorious as flesh risen again."[15] Beginning on the morning of the third day, Jesus's disciples began to see the glory that was preparing out of sight. They saw him in the flesh.

Resurrection: He Makes All Things New

What God restored in the darkness breaks forth on the morning of the third day. The secret of divine love is seen and heard. The ineffable mystery is made present to our senses. In the garden outside the tomb, on the way to Emmaus, in the upper room, on the seashore, and elsewhere, the disciples encounter Jesus Christ himself: Body and Blood, soul and divinity. "He has risen, as he said" (Mt 28:6).

The Death and Resurrection of Christ accomplish the glorious reunion of what was sorrowfully separated. He has claimed the dead in himself: he has become their life, restoring dominion, communion, and the union of their bodies and souls. But why, then, does Christ appear to his living disciples for forty days after Easter? Why does it matter that *they* should know that he has risen from the dead, and why does it matter that *we* should know this by way of their testimony?

It matters because the risen Christ makes himself the object of our faith and the substance of our hope. Though faith is challenging, he makes it reasonable because he allows his witnesses to see, hear, and touch him; and though hope is difficult, they can base it on the personal encounter with him risen from the dead. During those forty days, his witnesses encounter him as incarnate love, and that makes all the difference for them, as it may then for us who depend on their testimony. The witnesses to his Resurrection pass him on to us in word and sacrament.

According to John the Evangelist, the risen Lord appears to Mary of Magdala outside the tomb, early in the morning on the third day. Later that evening, Jesus comes among his disciples, who are locked away in the upper room. The last time they gathered around him, he gave them his Body and his Blood as the source of their communion in him, but immediately they began to break that solemn communion. Locked behind those doors now, do they not feel the utter pain of the separation they caused, the guilt of their abandonment, the shame of their hardness of heart? So now that he who was dead stands living among them, what does he say and do?

First, Jesus says to them, "Peace be with you" (Jn 20:19b). This is not peace as the world gives it, where discord is subdued by force. This peace is offered by the victim. Next, "he showed them his hands and his side" (Jn 20:20a). They see the marks that the sins of many, including their own sins, have left on his body. He bears the wounds of his Passion, and by these wounds, they not only recognize him but, strangely, are glad to see him (Jn 20:20b). These wounds—precisely where their pain, guilt, and shame ought to be most intense—are now the very source of their joy in his peace. The disciples are being refashioned by *his body*. Again he gives them his peace (Jn 20:21a), as if wrapping their wounds and his together in his peace. With this second offer of peace, he makes them partakers of his own mission from the Father: "'As the Father has sent me, even so I send you.' And when he had said this, he breathed on them, and said to them, 'Receive the Holy Spirit'" (Jn 20:21b–22). By his breath, the Spirit that unites him with the Father comes to fill and animate them, and as he has forgiven them, so they are commissioned to offer his forgiveness to others (20:23).

These actions Jesus performs are divine actions. He fashions the disciples anew from his own wounds. He breathes into them his own breath. He brings them into union through his own peace. He gives them a mission from his own mission—dominion from his absolute dominion. Irenaeus calls this work "the ancient formation of man,"[16] but here Jesus is making these disciples into a *new* creation. They who sinned, broke communion, abandoned their calling, and hid in fear now live in him. The gift of resurrection is not only for the dead but also for the living.

Jesus Christ is always himself. He who was among the dead is the same one who stands in the midst of his disciples on the evening of that first day of the week. They see him and hear him and touch him. As they gather around him, he is the one who unites them not only to each other and to those to whom he sends them but also to the dead whom this same Jesus claimed as his own in his descent in the grave. In seeing, hearing, and touching *him*, they encounter the "union . . . that is in no way interrupted" (*Lumen Gentium*, 49). He *is* that union: the union of the living and the dead.

SEEKING THE LIVING AMONG THE DEAD

One of the apostles was not there that evening when the Lord stood among the others: Thomas was elsewhere. He did not see or hear or touch the risen Christ, and so he will not believe. The others proclaim the Good News to him—"We have seen the Lord" (Jn 20:25)—but without having encountered him, Thomas remains in mourning.

Have you ever imagined the sorrow that Thomas alone among the apostles experienced for the week that followed? He grieved alone. He must have been tempted by their joy, but he would not accept it as his own. And the others must have been troubled by his persistent sorrow and perhaps even been tempted because of him to question their own joy.

It is only when they are all together again in the same house where Jesus broke bread with them the night before he died, and where he appeared to the other disciples but not to Thomas, that Thomas's lonely sorrow begins to heal. That house must have become for Thomas the site of double heartbreak: the place in his memory of his last communion with Jesus and then of his strange alienation from the new communion the others claimed to have found without Thomas. Then, right in that very place, the Lord comes to them again, and this time he calls to Thomas personally: "'Put your finger here, and see my hands; and put out your hand, and place it in my side; do not be faithless, but believing'" (Jn 20:27). Seeing and hearing Jesus, Thomas immediately "touches" him in an act of worship, proclaiming who this man Jesus is: "My Lord and my God!" (Jn 20:28). The crucified and risen Christ not only plunged into death to bring forth life, he also plunged into the deep places of Thomas's sorrow to bring forth joy.

The mere proclamation of the Good News was not enough for Thomas, nor is it enough for anyone who grieves. Thomas had to encounter the one who was proclaimed to him. He had to touch him in an act of worship. The descendants of Thomas are those of us who need to touch the risen Christ in the sacraments, and reach for him in devotions and bodily practices, so that we might know our union with our beloved dead through him who united himself with the dead. (We will pay attention to this more fully in chapter 4 and the epilogue.)

We ought not forget that well before the risen Christ appeared to Thomas, even before he appeared to the other apostles hiding in the upper room, he came to Mary of Magdala, who "stood weeping outside the tomb" (Jn 20:11). She went there in search of a dead body: the remnants of the one she loved. That very one appears to her alive, but she does not recognize him because she has been looking for him among the dead. Only when he calls her name is she shocked into recognition (Jn 20:16); we might imagine the pressure that builds and bursts within her as her enclosed sorrow is suddenly pierced by his voice. His next words to her seem strange: "'Do not hold on to me, for I have not yet ascended to my Father'" (Jn 20:17). Why shouldn't she hold on to him? Because, it seems, she wants to hold on to him as she has known him, rather than learning to love him as he is, for who he is. She wants to claim him as her own, not follow him into union with his Father. Like the apostles who will meet the risen Christ after her, Mary of Magdala must be remade in his glorious image.[17]

The descendants of Mary of Magdala are those of us who, like Stephanie DePrez, hold the bodies of those we love and know they are not there, who reach for the presence of someone painfully absent but cannot find them. Mary of Magdala wants her beloved to come back to where she is, but the Lord tells her that she must go to where he is. This is the challenge for us whom death separates from those we love: we must learn how to seek them in Christ. It is an arduous search, and it requires all we have.

Mary, the mother of Jesus, is the first to follow her son into his Father's household. In her glorious Assumption, she follows the path of his Ascension. Heaven is union with him where he is. She who held his lifeless body in the dust beneath the Cross beholds him in everlasting glory.

2.

HEAVEN AND THE HORIZON OF HOPE

On Saturday night, Laura Kelly Fanucci gave birth to twin girls: Maggie and Abby. On Sunday afternoon, Laura and her husband, Franco, held tiny Maggie in their arms as she died. On Monday, they awoke knowing that before day's end, they would have to do the same with Abby.

When the hour arrived, the nurse asked Laura if she would like to hold Abby skin to skin before they started to disconnect the tubes from her daughter. Weighed down by the grief of the previous day and dreading the new loss she would soon bear, Laura reclined in her chair and opened her arms. The nurse laid Abby across her mother's chest. Here, in Laura's words, is what happened next: "I started to smile. I started to *grin*. This is not the reaction you expect when nurses place your dying baby to your skin. But everything turned inside out. I was flooded with peace. I was filled with the deepest joy I have ever felt. I could not understand why sorrow and grief had occupied any inch of my body before that instant. This was a different world."[1]

In the book of Revelation, after the visionary has seen all the tumult and tribulation of this world come to an end, he beholds the vision of a new world where God is all in all: "He will wipe away every tear from their eyes, and there shall be no more death or mourning, wailing or pain, for the old order has passed away" (Rev 21:4, NAB). Our world had not ended for Laura, nor was her child saved from death. And yet the only way Laura could describe what she and Franco experienced as they took turns holding Abby's fragile body against their own bodies was that this was "heaven stretched out for hours."[2]

This fullness of life at the hour of death was bewildering. Even while it was happening, Laura recognized the inexplicableness of it all—and somehow she started to remember her previous day of grief differently: "After twenty, thirty, forty minutes of unrelenting joy, I started to wonder why there was no dip in the surge. Why I could not conjure a single sentiment of sadness. Why I could not remember why I had wept when we said goodbye to Maggie, when we knew this perfect joy was what awaited her."[3]

Joy was working backward: *every* tear was being wiped away. But where did this joy come from? Nothing was different from the day before, when Laura and Franco had felt only grief at the death of Maggie. This joy just suddenly arrived the moment Laura and Abby touched skin-to-skin and persisted as long as Laura or Franco held Abby close to them. Within this joy, there was no sorrow. Even now, years after that inexplicable day, even as they grieve the death of their daughters, the joy remains indelibly etched in their memories.[4]

"We were right inside the heart of God," Laura recalls.[5] By her testimony, the heart of God is a place of communion: she and Franco were in intimate union with their daughter in that sacred space. They experienced what might well be a foretaste of our bodily resurrection, where physical bodies, sown as perishable, dishonorable, and weak, are raised as spiritual bodies: imperishable, glorious, and powerful (see 1 Corinthians 15:42–44). When we are together in that way, there shall be knowledge and love, fullness and peace, presence and communion. That is the horizon of Christian hope.

Laura's testimony challenges commonplace notions of heaven. Oftentimes, we imagine heaven as a place we get to.[6] What Laura described as heaven was instead the fullness of presence, peace, and communion. This aligns brilliantly with what the Church professes about heaven: it is not so much a place as union with God in Christ and with all the others who live in him. Joseph Ratzinger (Pope Benedict XVI) indicates a revolution of desire when he writes,

> Christian hope is not some news item about tomorrow or the day after tomorrow. We might put it this way: hope is now personalized. Its focus is not space and time, the questions of "Where?" and "When?," but relationship with Christ's person and longing for him to come close.[7]

Heaven is the fulfillment of that longing—that desire for intimacy. Without expecting it or even being able to explain it, Laura and Franco experienced a foretaste of that fulfillment with their beloved daughter Abby. They longed for that fulfillment for their other beloved daughter, Maggie, believing that "this perfect joy was what awaited her."[8] Such joy is neither made nor achieved; it is given.

When Christ appeared to his disciples in the glory of the Resurrection, he brought the fulfillment of this hope near to them. When he ascended to his Father, he beckoned his disciples to the fullness of his joy. Those of us who remain below do not yet know what we or our faithful departed shall be, "but we know that when [Christ] appears we shall be like him" (1 Jn 3:2).

In the introduction to this book, I said that I want to help awaken the Christian imagination and to do that we have to imagine communion. In the previous chapter, we contemplated the source of our communion in Christ: his Passion, Death, and Resurrection. In this chapter, we set our gaze on what Christ promises to us: that we shall become like him. This requires us to follow the Fanuccis' invitation to reimagine heaven by heeding the decisiveness of Christ's Ascension. We will then learn from scripture and tradition what our becoming like Christ will entail in the resurrection of our bodies, principally through the four properties of glorified bodies. From there, with the help of Jonathan Edwards, we will better be able to articulate and indeed *imagine* what exactly we hope for when we long for the life and the presence of our beloved dead.

Imagining is not the same as reunion or communion. But without the right imagining, our practices of communion are sure to go astray. If we do not strain to know what we seek, then we are not likely to know how to seek. Reimagining heaven in fidelity to Christ is an utterly practical matter: he is our hope, and he shows us how to hope, today and always.

THE ASCENSION: HEAVEN MADE PERSONAL

Weeping outside the tomb, Mary of Magdala does not desire enough. When the Lord calls her name and she is shocked into recognizing him, she still does not desire enough. She is only as yet prepared to behold him where and as she is. She has not yet been awakened to the desire to follow him into the fullness of joy.

Yes, the Son of God became one with us, even sharing in our death. And yes, he rose and returned to meet those who longed for him. But his mission was not complete in becoming one with us and joining us. His mission is complete in uniting us, with him, to his Father. He, who is the Son of God, became like us so that we might become like him.[9] He descended to raise us with him to his Father's house.[10] What was true for Mary of Magdala is true for us: *we* too are called to follow Christ's Ascension.

Mary of Magdala gazes upon a glorified human body. The body of the risen Christ reveals the humanity the Son of God shares with us, now made perfect in union with his heavenly Father. With her own eyes, Mary sees the glory of heaven, but heaven is still beyond her. For Mary of Magdala to enjoy heaven, she herself will have to be changed to become like Christ is. She cannot hold on to him, but must follow him into his Father's house (see John 14:1–4).

In his classic work on the mystery of God, *De Trinitate*, St. Augustine teaches the necessity of this movement toward the Father. With Mary of Magdala in mind, Augustine speaks of the movement of disciples from knowing Christ as he lived among them in this world to following Christ as he ascends to the Father:

> It was necessary for the form of a servant to be removed from their sight, since as long as they could observe it they would think that Christ was this only which they had before their eyes. . . . It also explains that other text, *Do not touch me, for I have not yet ascended to the Father* (Jn 20:17). Touching concludes as it were the process of getting acquainted. He did

> not want [Mary of Magdala's] heart, so eagerly reach-
> ing out to him, to stop at thinking that he was only
> what could be seen and touched. His ascension to
> the Father signified his being seen in his equality
> with the Father, that being the ultimate vision which
> suffices us.[11]

To stop short of following Christ who ascends is to miss out on what God intends for us. We are to be made perfect in his love, living fully with him and in him. This is not just the call for each of us individually but indeed for all of us together. Mary of Magdala was the first to receive Christ's demanding and liberating call: do not seek to keep me here where you are, but follow me into the fullness of joy.

Just as the rediscovery of Christian hope requires us to contemplate more fully the Passion, Death, and Resurrection of Christ, it also requires a renewed contemplation of the Ascension of Christ. But this contemplation does not end with watching Christ ascend; rather, it requires us to grasp and heed how we are called to rise with him and therefore how we are to entrust our faithful departed to the hope his Ascension opens for us. This means opening ourselves to the truth that the Ascension was not completed all at once, nor is it only coming in the future. For Christians, the Ascension is happening now. Theologian and liturgist Jean Corbon expresses this mystery beautifully:

> Jesus is, of course, at his Father's side. If, however,
> we reduce this "ascent" to a particular moment in
> our mortal history, we simply forget that beginning
> with the hour of his Cross and Resurrection, Jesus
> and the human race are henceforth one. He became

> a son of man in order that we might become sons of God. The Ascension is progressive "until we all . . . form the perfect Man fully mature with the fullness of Christ himself" (Ephesians 4:13). The movement of the Ascension will be complete only when all the members of his body have been drawn to the Father and brought to life by his Spirit.[12]

Christ's Ascension is complete when we join him. When Laura Fanucci speaks of experiencing "heaven stretched out for hours" while holding her daughter Abby, she testifies to a kind of relation and communion that transforms all other forms of relating. This joy did not happen *outside* of the body or aside from our humanity; rather, it was communicated fully in and through our humanity. As Laura testifies, the experience seemed to transfigure this life, now, in terms of what to hope for and what to desire. This foretaste of unending joy was thus a calling—a beckoning— to glory we have not yet known but which is prepared for us. The path by which that calling comes is the path of Christ's Ascension. He goes to his Father so that where he is we may also be. But to be "there" with him is not to arrive at some "place"—it is instead to join in his union with his Father. It means becoming like him, so that our humanity may be glorified. Heaven is the "space" of full relation and communion, in Christ.

Saints do not go to heaven; they go to Christ—their communion in him *is* heaven. On our own, we cannot imagine the degree of intimacy and union that comes with this perfection of "being with Christ" and "being with one another in Christ." We are far too weighed down by our failures in loving, our limitations in expressing and receiving love, and our weakness in constantly willing the good of others. We fear loss, we cling to our comforts, and we are sluggish in letting go of our preferences. And some more than others bear the wounds of others' lack of love for us—the cruelties we have endured—which make the vulnerability and transparency of true union virtually unimaginable. To imagine heaven as communion in Christ, we have to imagine being freed *from* all that, freed *for* the love Christ intends for us. We have to imagine ourselves and each other not as we presently are but as we will become in him. Thus, our hope for heaven always begins with Christ: he shows us what glorified humanity looks like, both so that we can know him and so that we can glimpse what we are to become.

WHAT WE SHALL BECOME, IN GLORY

Christ's glorified body was glimpsed by those still in this world. For forty days "he appeared to Cephas [Peter], then to the twelve. Then he appeared to more than five hundred brethren at one time. . . . Then he appeared to James, then to all the apostles. Last of all . . . he appeared also to [Paul]" (1 Cor 15:5–8). According to St. John, he appeared to Mary of Magdala outside the tomb, and according to St. Luke, he appeared to two disciples on their way to a town called Emmaus. From all these witnesses, we receive unusual accounts. Jesus is truly present, but initially they cannot recognize him (Jn 20:14, 21:4; Lk 24:16). He appears within locked rooms (Jn 20:19). His apostles think him to be "a spirit" and are at first frightened (Lk 24:37), and yet he has flesh and bones and the marks of his Crucifixion, and he eats with them (Lk 24:42; Jn 20:20, 21:12–13). It is he, but not as his disciples expected him to be.

The Only Begotten Son of the Father who becomes flesh, dies, and rises from the dead is, as his witnesses behold, truly human. He appears to them as they have known him: bodily. But what is new is how he is revealed to them when sin and death no longer stand between their deepest desire and the Son of God who loves them. Before them is Jesus Christ—fully human, fully divine—whose humanity is the perfect instrument of divine glory. In him, they see what their own humanity was created to be and has now become.

Contemplating the biblical witness to the Resurrection, the Church seeks to understand the glorious revelation of humanity in the risen Christ. This theological reflection begins when St. Paul, in his First Letter to the Corinthians, proclaims that "Christ has been raised from the dead" and is therefore "the first fruits of those who have fallen asleep" (1 Cor 15:20). In the course of his teaching on the resurrection of the dead based on faith in Christ's own Resurrection, Paul speaks of four marks of the transformation of human beings who die and are raised again to share in Christ's Resurrection: "What is sown is perishable, what is raised is imperishable. It is sown in dishonor, it is raised in glory. It is sown in weakness, it is raised in power. It is sown a physical body, it is raised a spiritual body" (1 Cor 15:42–44).

These four marks of transformation—called impassibility, subtlety, agility, and clarity—come together to attract our hope as magnetic north attracts the needle of a compass.

Impassibility

"What is sown is perishable, what is raised is imperishable."

I intend to be generous, until there is only one chocolate macaroon left and I am alone at the cupboard. I know that to be generous would mean forgoing the sudden urge to consume so that my wife or one of my children might enjoy what I myself am compelled to enjoy. It is as if I suddenly have two wills: one that pulls me toward generosity and another that pulls me toward this sweet. Alas, in the moment of crisis, I find myself living into St. Paul's confession: "I can will what is right, but I cannot do it. For I do not do the good I want" (Rom 7:18–19). The macaroon is delicious, but soon, the pleasure passes and guilt replaces it.

In experiences like this one and much more serious ones besides, we know the feeling of being at war with ourselves. The soul wills one thing, but the body leads us to another. We lack stability; it is as if our principle of action—our primary motivation—is regularly shifting. Even more, we know how our will slackens when our bodies tire, age, or are deprived of sleep or nutrients or health. We are subject to swirling passions.

Our bodies resurrected in the glory of Christ will be healed of this chronic instability. The body will be fitted perfectly into harmony with the soul, which shall give the body its form and its unchanging principle of action. This is what it means for the glorified body to enter into impassibility.

St. Thomas Aquinas expresses this particular perfection of the body like so: "Now the human body and all that it contains will be perfectly subject to the rational soul, even as the soul will be perfectly subject to God. Wherefore it will be impossible for the glorified body to be subject to any change contrary to the disposition whereby it is perfected by the soul; and consequently bodies will be impassible."[13]

In regard to the conflict in our will as between the desire to be generous and the desire to eat the last chocolate macaroon, we are now subject to passions, which, though influenced by what is outside of us, pull on us from within. We "suffer" these passions. But there is another way in which we suffer now, and that is through afflictions that come upon us from outside ourselves— we do not choose these afflictions. At various times or, for some, through longer seasons or the course of a lifetime, we are struck by infirmity, illness, or other impediments to our abilities. We feel in our mortal bodies the aches that come from aging. Our bodies fail us. Thinking in this way brings us to the other side of impassibility: freedom from these afflictions we suffer. The perfected, glorified body is no longer subject to these injuries.[14]

When they meet the risen Christ, the disciples pass back and forth from fear to peace, from guilt to joy. They are caught in the memory of what they have done and what they have failed to do, and they are subject to influence from the threats around them. They continue to go back to their old ways even as the Lord calls them forward into the stability and everlasting security of living in him. His life is to be their life: "Abide in me" is his constant refrain (see John 15:4–11).

Impassibility is a mark of the perfection of our bodies in Christ, the reliability of the body in union with the soul. In resurrected glory, our bodies will have but one master—the soul—and the soul will be obedient to God. This harmony shall be our final and permanent state.

Subtlety

"It is sown a physical body, it is raised a spiritual body."

When you burn your finger, I do not cry in pain. Your pain is your own, and I am separate from it. Likewise, when your heart breaks, I can move toward understanding and feeling with you, but there is always a barrier between what might be my desire to share completely in what you are experiencing and my ability to do so. The same is true when you experience joy, relief, or consolation that is distinctly your own: I may experience my own gladness at your good, but I am always separated from your good in some way. Those who love each other seek a union that escapes them. In this life, the seeking is itself the better part of love.

What you communicate to me of your experience is, of course, never a perfect expression (we will touch on this below with "clarity"). But it is at least equally true that the sensitivity of my discernment is also imperfect. My senses betray me, my methods of interpretation are fallible, and my ability to know you as you are is radically incomplete. I lack subtlety.

What is more, I lack of subtlety not only in my relation to you but also and especially in my relation to God, who is the source of my life and who is my fulfillment. I do not see him as I ought, I do not listen to his Word with all my might, and I am not sensitized to what he delights in. It is like trying to enjoy a symphony with a migraine, or attempting to relish a sumptuous feast while battling morning sickness (or so I hear).

What, then, comes from the property of subtlety in the glorified body? We might imagine it in this way: "As the soul enjoying God shall perfectly adhere to Him, and share in His goodness to the full height of its capacity; so the body shall be perfectly subject to the soul, and share in its attributes so far as possible, in clearness of sense, in seemliness of bodily appetite, and in general perfection of the entire organism."[15]

Our lack of subtlety in knowing and loving one another shall be cured. Mary of Magdala heard the Lord speak her name outside the tomb, but she interpreted his meaning imperfectly; Christ had to lead her forward into a new way of knowing. The proclamation of the Resurrection was not enough for Thomas, who relied on proof rather than trust; he was still coming to know the Lord as he is. Even as he walked beside them, the two on their way to Emmaus were prevented from seeing or hearing or remembering or hoping in Christ as he is; they were as yet desensitized to him.

St. John, in his first epistle, speaks to the perfection of our sensitivities, first of all in relation to knowing Christ: "When he appears we shall be like him, for we shall see him as he is" (1 Jn 3:2). We shall behold his glory, and in him we shall know and love each other, for we shall be made capable of that fullness of subtlety that presently eludes us.

Agility

"It is sown in weakness, it is raised in power."

"Daddy, again!" my daughter cries as she falls back into my arms from her upward launch. She laughs and delights, and I do, too . . . until the pain in my lower back pinches, my breathing begins to labor, and I get a little dizzy from the four, then eight, then God-knows-how-many tosses into the air. My spirit is willing, but my flesh is weak—very weak. And achy. And tired. And just not as capable of this as I was more than a decade ago when our firstborn was this little girl's size.

My body is moving toward death. Try as I might to sustain my body, I will lose vitality. I cannot do what I want, or what others want from me. Even if my principle of action were constant (impassible), my ability to follow through on that principle would, now, be wanting. I cannot communicate and follow through on the love I wish to express because my skill and aptitude in all manner of language—verbal, bodily, emotional—is not up to the task.

Living wholly from God in the resurrection will complete what is now lacking in my vital power. This body of mine will be filled with the power to do what I ought to do and most deeply desire to do. As St. Thomas puts it, "The soul that shall enjoy the vision of God, being conjoined to its last end, will find its desire fulfilled in all things. And because the body moves at the desire of the soul, the body in this case will absolutely obey the beck of the spirit in its every command to move: hence the bodies of the risen will be agile."[16]

It is difficult not only to imagine but even to describe this perfected agility. We may catch glimpses of it, though most of us are more familiar with the frustrations of not being able to do what we would like to do. To appeal to our imaginations, then, Paul Claudel speaks of agility in musical terms:

> Agility is that endowment which enables the individual to . . . instantly assume a certain outward form in the scheme of things, in an ever-fresh harmonic and melodic relationship with this scheme, a relationship begotten of the endless necessities of love. Distance for him is no longer a separation or a removal, but what in the language of music is called an interval. In praising God, he passes over all of paradise in a marvelous sonority, as the bow passes over the string; and it is impossible to tell if he is singing, or if everything is vibrating in his wake.[17]

We might also find glimmers of this perfected agility in the movements of a superior athlete, as David Foster Wallace did when watching the Swiss tennis star Roger Federer:

> A top athlete's beauty is next to impossible to describe directly. Or to evoke. Federer's forehand is a great liquid whip, his backhand a one-hander that he can drive flat, load with topspin, or slice—the slice with such snap that the ball turns shapes in the air and skids on the grass to maybe ankle height. His serve has world-class pace and a degree of placement and variety no one else comes close to; the service motion is lithe and uneccentric, distinctive (on TV) only in a certain eel-like all-body snap at the moment of impact. His anticipation and court sense are otherworldly, and his footwork is the best in the game. . . . All this is true, and yet none of it really explains anything or evokes the experience of watching this man play. Of witnessing, firsthand, the beauty and genius of his game.[18]

Perhaps the best way to imagine or describe the glorified body's agility is to observe children. Children do not tire. They do what they seek to do, and they do it over and over again. For the aging adult, the child is a marvel more distant than the most distant memory of oneself. "I was never *that* young," the old man says. That might come closest to the degree of difference between the fleeting moments of imperfect agility we experience now and the unbounded agility promised to us in the resurrection.[19]

The apostles who first encountered the risen Lord could not communicate any better what had taken place than to say, "We have seen the Lord" (Jn 20:25). Their words were insufficient to the mystery, and Thomas was unconvinced. Later, though Peter was filled with the desire to love the Lord, he was sluggish in being able to follow through, tainted as he was by the memory of his denials of Christ. To make up for the power of love he lacked, he would have to learn to love through suffering for the Lord's sake, heeding the Lord's command to "follow me" into the fullness of resurrected life (see John 21:15–19). The gifts the Lord bestows upon those who are raised to live fully in him include the power to completely embody the love of God.

Clarity

"It is sown in dishonor, it is raised in glory."

"If you hadn't told me what was going on with him, I would have never known," my childhood next-door neighbor said to his mom, in reference to me at the age of seven. She had told him that my parents were getting divorced and that this was very hard for me. But what I showed on the outside was not a clear or accurate representation of what my friend's mom told him. I was opaque; I often am.

Rather than aspire to full transparency, most of us more often have nightmares about other people seeing us as we are. Social media profiles are carefully curated. College application essays project a preferred version of ourselves. Job applications tell an unblemished narrative. We are used to seeking admiration but at the same time fear disgrace should we be seen just as we are. To be perceived as ordinary is perhaps the worst fate of all.

True intimacy is rare and not easily realized. Over time and step by step along a path of hesitating trust, the courage to be vulnerable sometimes thickens. Yet even when no greater trust between two people could be imagined, there are still hesitations, and doubts creep in unannounced. To be able to show another person who and what I really am seems all but impossible.

What would it mean to appear as we really are? It would mean that the defensive postures we consciously and subconsciously assume would fall away. It would mean that the "unfortunate default face" many of us are cursed with would be transformed, so that a scowl would only appear when it should. There would be only truth: I would be true to myself and true to you. Being seen would mean being instantly known. This all sounds a little (perhaps very) terrifying . . . until we add the final part to our question: What would it mean to appear as we really are *in God*?

Clarity as it pertains to the glorified body means that the brightness of divine knowledge and love would fill us and shine from us. This is based, again, on the harmony of the soul with God, and of the body with the soul. St. Thomas explains it like this:

> From the brightness and excellence of the soul that is raised to the vision of God, the body, united to such a soul, shall gain a further advantage. It will be entirely subject to the soul, God's power so disposing, not in being only, but in all its actions, experiences, motions and bodily qualities. As then the soul in the enjoyment of the vision of God will be replenished with a spiritual brightness, so by an overflow from soul to body, the body itself, in its way, will be clad in a halo and glory of brightness.[20]

This clarity—or "brightness"—does not mean that the individuality of a particular person is erased. On the contrary, the brightness of God's love shining through the whole person without opposition or impediment reveals each person's particularity in all its fullness, both to the person and to others (see Psalm 139). In the glory of the resurrection, sins are forgiven and their wounds healed. The real and imagined reasons for shame are cured. What remains is the whole person, truly alive for the first time. "For the glory of God is a living man," St. Irenaeus comments, "and the life of man consists in beholding God."[21] (When Irenaeus speaks of "man" or a "living man," he always has in mind "the whole man"—that is, the union of body and soul, in harmony with God.)

We again turn to Paul Claudel to discover a hint of the particular, unique, unrepeatable, and unbound beauty of a glorified human person: "The light which proceeds from each of us, albeit kindled at a single source is, insofar as it represents individual testimony, of infinite variety. This is why the Bible compares the righteous to the stars without number, which differ from one another in size and quality and which God nevertheless knows and calls like sheep, each by its own name."[22] Said another way, the beautiful variety of flowers in the field is in no way diminished because they are all revealed by the light of a single source: the one sun shining down from above.

To overcome our lingering terror of this promised revelation, the glorious light of the Lord must also heal and strengthen. To reveal us to ourselves and one another in our sin-laden weakness, or with the unhealed marks of others' sins upon us, would be no mercy at all. That would be a revelation for the condemned, not the saved. So it is, therefore, that clarity also comes with courage. Those who are glorified in the Lord take on *his* strength as their own:

> The LORD is my light and my salvation;
> whom shall I fear?
> The LORD is the stronghold of my life;
> of whom shall I be afraid? (Ps 27:1)

The Glorified One

"We have beheld his glory, glory as of the only Son from the Father" (Jn 1:14).

The unimaginable glory of the dead who are resurrected into the life of Christ is imaginable because it has been revealed. The risen Christ appeared to his chosen witnesses; they testify to him as the source of our hope. His glory is to become our own.

Christ himself reveals the *impassibility* of human flesh glorified in him: "I am ascending to my Father and your Father, to my God and your God" (Jn 20:17). The harmony of God and God's creatures is secured in Jesus Christ, risen and ascended, who joins us in calling upon his Father as "God" and brings us to join him in calling our God "Father." This is the utter stability of union in solidarity.

Christ himself reveals the *subtlety* of human flesh glorified in him. He walks right through the locked doors of his disciples' fear (Jn 20:19); he sees into the depths of Thomas's sorrow and doubt (Jn 20:26–29); he perceives the hidden shame and guilt of Peter's denial of him at the hour of his Passion (Jn 21:15–17); and he reads the hearts of the two wanderers bound for Emmaus who had lost hope (Lk 24:13–35, especially 17, 21, and 32). This is the mercy of God perfectly channeled through human flesh.

Christ himself reveals the *agility* of human flesh glorified in him. With the gift of the bread that he takes, blesses, breaks, and gives to the two disciples in Emmaus, he fills them with the zeal to arise and move in haste (Lk 24:30–35). With authority, he proclaims his disciples as his witnesses and sends "the promise of my Father" upon them, to clothe them "with power from on high" (Lk 24:48–49). By the power of his words he changes his wounds from the source of pain and sorrow to the source of forgiveness for his disciples, when twice he says "Peace be with you" (Jn 20:19, 21). Then by the power of his breath, he gives them the Holy Spirit and empowers them to judge and forgive (Jn 20:22–23). He commands the failing disciples to cast out their nets again to find the fish they seek, rekindling their memories of his initial call to them and thereby helping them to know him again (Jn 21:4–8). In Christ's bodily encounters with his disciples, he begins to transfer the power of God to them through his actions.

And Christ himself reveals the *clarity* of human flesh glorified in him. When he shows his hands and his side to his disciples, they know him and are glad (Jn 20:20–21; Lk 24:36–42). Even more, Thomas proclaims Christ's true identity when he gazes upon him: "My Lord and my God!" (Jn 20:28). To the eyes of those who love him, Christ is known immediately: John, the beloved disciple, "said to Peter, 'It is the Lord!'" (Jn 21:7). The two disciples at Emmaus tell "how he was known to them in the breaking of the bread" (Lk 24:35). By the light of his Resurrection, Christ's disciples begin to see, know, and love him truly, moving past their own previous failures in intimacy. By his glorified body, Christ shows them all exactly who he is.

He is the Word who became flesh and dwelt among us, who goes ahead to prepare a place for us, so that where he is—*as he is*—we may also be (Jn 1:14, 14:3).

HEAVEN IS A WORLD OF LOVE

Reading of the risen Christ's appearances to his disciples during the forty days before his Ascension, we might find some sense of frustration rather than consolation. He appeared to *them*, not to *us*. We might feel cheated: How can the risen Christ be the foundation of our hope if we have not encountered him as his first disciples did?

Moreover, upon the death of a loved one, few have experienced the joy that enveloped Laura and Franco Fanucci when holding their dying daughter Abby. It is more common to experience the sheer grief Laura and Franco felt when holding their dying daughter Maggie. After she shared her story about Abby in writing, Laura began receiving messages from others thanking her for her beautiful testimony; some said they had experienced something similar. But Laura received other messages from grieving parents who were dismayed at not experiencing the joy the Fanuccis experienced, and who wondered what they had done wrong. In response, Laura wrote again:

> I do not know why there are unexpected glimpses of grace in certain places, not others. What happened to us was strange and shocking and unbidden. We still talk about it every day because it made no sense to us. It still wakes me up at night, and I do not understand what it means. . . . But if you have had to sit in the dark and the worst and the terrible depths, and you wonder why it didn't happen to you, I want to tell you that we know the anger of emptiness, too. **We have been on the dark side of light.**

> When Maggie died, we did not experience light and joy. We were shattered. I felt like my heart had been physically ripped out of my chest and left to bleed.
>
> When we lost a baby to miscarriage three years ago, there was no peace. No heaven. It was pure hell. Desolation without consolation.[23]

How do you believe in the joy of heaven when the experience of the death of loved ones is mostly grief, agony, and sorrow? Those who have not experienced the joy the Fanuccis knew with Abby might think that hope would be possible only if they had such an experience; without that experience, many of us might sense no foundation for our hope.

To eighteenth-century Christians who similarly felt that their loved ones were just gone, the Congregationalist pastor Jonathan Edwards preached on heaven as a world of love. He preached on the basis not of a direct experience of this joy but from his contemplation of heaven according to the biblical testimony. He preached, therefore, from the position of faith—not certainty—about "things not seen" (Heb 11:1), inviting his listeners to join him in this contemplation.

Edwards begins by presenting to his listeners' imagination what he glimpses in his own imagination, formed as it is by the divine scriptures: "My mind was very much taken up with contemplations of heaven, and the enjoyments there; and living there in perfect holiness, humility and love. . . . Heaven appeared exceedingly delightful, as a world of love; and . . . all happiness consisted in living in pure, humble, heavenly, divine love."[24]

This sounds unspecific and wishful. We suspect "a world of love" to be more like a utopian dream than a reality reckoning with the sting of death that separates loved ones. As Edwards continues, though, he brings this pain of separation to the fore as his listeners no doubt call to mind their own beloved dead:

> [E]very gem which death rudely tears away from us here is a glorious jewel forever shining there; every Christian friend that goes before us from this world, is a ransomed spirit waiting to welcome us in heaven. There will be the infant of days that we have lost below, through grace to be found above; there the Christian father, and mother, and wife, and child, and friend, with whom we shall renew the holy fellowship of the saints, which was interrupted by death here, but shall be commenced again in the upper sanctuary, and then shall never end.[25]

Having recalled the particular persons whom his congregants personally grieve, Edwards seems now to promise a restoration of what has been lost. It sounds as if life will go on—in heaven—as it did here on earth before death "interrupted" fellowship. This is likely what many would want: to have those who have died returned to us as they were, so that we might enjoy again the relationship that has been ruptured. But Edwards does not let the desires of his listeners settle on the familiar—no, the point of this sermon is to stretch his listeners forward in faith. The matter at hand is to reimagine who our beloved dead are as saints.

He goes on: "That which was in the heart on earth as but a grain of mustard-seed, shall be as a great tree in heaven. The soul that in this world had only a little spark of divine love in it, in heaven shall be, as it were, turned into a bright and ardent flame, like the sun in its fullest brightness, when it has no spot upon it."[26] Those whom we have known and loved in this life we have only known and loved partially, imperfectly. In heaven, what has been partial shall be made complete, and what has been imperfect shall be perfected. We do not abandon what we have known of or how we have loved those we grieve, but we must not confine them to our terms. Edwards is flipping things around: heaven is the true reality, and earth must be reseen in light of heaven. St. Paul, in his discourse on love, puts the matter this way: "For now we see in a mirror dimly, but then face to face. Now I know in part; then I shall understand fully, even as I have been fully understood" (1 Cor 13:12).

To move from the dim mirror to the true image, Edwards leads his listeners to reimagine their beloved dead: "The saints in heaven shall have no difficulty in expressing all their love. Their souls being on fire with holy love shall not be like a fire pent up, but like a flame uncovered and at liberty. Their spirits, being winged with love, shall have no weight upon them to hinder their flight. There shall be no want of strength or activity, nor any want of words wherewith to praise the object of their affection."[27] In these brief lines, Edwards proposes to his listeners the properties of the glorified resurrected body. "Being on fire with holy love" speaks to impassibility: divine love is the one, constant, and secure principle by which the blessed move. "Like a flame uncovered and at liberty" speaks to subtlety: the light and the heat of each blessed soul touches everything through the glorified body, without hindrance from within or from the outside, so they will understand fully and completely. "There shall be no want of strength or activity" speaks to agility: freed from the "weight" of a body bound for death and with a body resurrected with the power of God, the blessed are capable of doing what they desire to do in love—encounter others fully. Finally, "no difficulty in expressing all their love" speaks to clarity: what each of the blessed are is what they show themselves to be—they are made known by their love, so their bodies will reveal what their souls have become, "a bright and ardent flame."

Imagining our departed loved ones in these terms is a demanding task. Seeking for the beloved dead in heaven requires us to move beyond the imperfect and partial ways we have known and been known, loved and been loved, in the past. This image of heaven is thus at once consoling and piercing. Imagining one's own beloved dead in heavenly bliss is consoling, as is the promise of being united to them again, but to begin to imagine them rightly we must pierce through what we think we know and what we previously desired. The beloved dead have gone to Christ, to become as he is; we cannot find them by making them once again as we are now. Edwards puts his listeners in the same position as the disciples encountering the risen Christ in those first forty days: they cannot cling to what they have expected and desired, but must grow toward the fullness of all joy. It is more than any of us has wanted.

Edwards's sermon gives us the chance to reconsider experiences of inexplicable joy like the Fanuccis'. Rather than private experiences of the fortunate few, these are instead images meant to incline those of us who have not "seen" to contemplate what has been promised in Christ. As Laura says, she has seen both inexplicable joy and unmitigated sorrow. For all Christians who hope for their loved ones upon death, the challenge is the same: to trust that what Christ has promised and revealed in himself is true reality, in the light of which we are to reimagine even our world and our lives now.

For Catholic Christians, the glory of the risen Christ is passed on not only through preaching but also and especially through sacrament. Through the Eucharist, the good news of the glorious Resurrection of Christ moves beyond hearing and thinking, and into receiving and sensing. Quoting St. Irenaeus, the *Catechism of the Catholic Church* instructs that "just as bread that comes from the earth, after God's blessing has been invoked upon it, is no longer ordinary bread, but Eucharist, formed of two things, the one earthly and the other heavenly: so too our bodies, which partake of the Eucharist, are no longer corruptible, but possess the hope of resurrection" (*CCC*, 1000).[28] The only way to "possess hope" is to strive forward toward what hope points to—in this case, the union of our bodies with the glorified body of Christ. And so it is that the call to those who receive the Eucharist is the same as it was to those first disciples—to forgo trying to "hold on to" him as we are now or as we expect him to be. Instead, we are called to stretch forward to where he is, at home in his Father's house, with all those who are raised in him.

3.

LOSS AND THE LONGING FOR WHOLENESS

Sitting on the floor, Robert Cording stares at pictures of his son Daniel on his wedding day. Daniel had arranged these photos in a frame he constructed out of an old window pane for his wife, Leisl. After Daniel died, Leisl gave the gift to Daniel's parents. Gazing at the photos of his beloved, deceased son, Robert lets himself be "concussed in tears."

"Perhaps," he writes, "grief is an attempt to hit a note that would shatter this world like glass and allow me to walk through the barrier that keeps my son apart from me for all my remaining days."[1] Robert holds this grief; he does not hide from it. He does not want his son to be dead, but also does not want the grief over his son's death to leave him. He wants to feel the absence because in feeling the absence, he feels his son.

Daniel remains Robert's son; Robert remains Daniel's father. Life is changed, not ended, for Robert, who lives as Daniel's father now in a way that is different—painfully different—from how he lived as Daniel's father "before." Daniel's absence matters absolutely, and Robert heeds Daniel's absence as a calling—a calling to allow Daniel to be present in his life, now: "Daniel's presence calls to something in me to answer. It is as if his loss, his utter absence, has to be part of my ongoing life. I sense him as an absolute hole in my life that I must accept. And I have to carry that absence around with me, and if I can be present to that absence, it helps me to be whole."[2]

Wholeness, it seems, is not the same as contentment or comfort. Rather, wholeness is a matter of truth—the truth that you are not yourself by yourself. The whole of Robert Cording is bound up with his son Daniel, just as the whole of Robert Cording is bound up with his other two (living) sons, and his wife, and his friends and neighbors. But these people are not interchangeable parts, and no one is a substitute for anyone else. This is never more apparent to Robert than with his son Daniel. For Robert, there is no substitute for Daniel. Daniel is his son— the one who is absent, whose presence Robert seeks, even if now mostly by longing.

There is something disorienting in what Robert brings to the fore. He is not trying to bring his son back to where he himself is: "I am not delusional," Robert says, "nor am I denying his death."[3] Daniel will not live again in the same way Robert knew his son previously. Even more, Robert is not projecting onto his son some wish for closure or consolation. Instead, Robert holds on to Daniel's absence and, in this way, holds his son as part of what it means for him, Robert, to be wholly himself.

Robert desires the presence of his son as his son should be: alive, bodily. At the cost of pain and persistent longing, Robert is allowing himself to be changed for love of his son. To do this, Robert neither denies death nor allows death to keep him from his son. He seeks to love his son from here.

Perhaps, though, Robert is not the only one in this relationship who is seeking and longing. What if Daniel, too, is seeking and longing, not just for final rest in God but also for communion with his father, with his mother, with his wife and friends and neighbors? What if the desire to be one goes in both directions? What if the desire from the side of the beloved dead is even greater? The Christian hope for heaven and the doctrine of purgatory command us to grapple with such overwhelming thoughts. As we do so, we begin to reckon with the possibility that our grief over the absence of our beloved dead is, in a significant way, a response to their longing for us.

In the last chapter, we sought to imagine the horizon of Christian hope in the Ascension of Christ and in the properties of glorified bodies made capable of the fullness of relationship. Now we take up the challenge presented to us at the close of that chapter—the challenge to begin reimagining our world and our lives *now* in light of the hope of perfect communion, especially between us who are living and the faithful who have died. This act of imagination forces us to reckon more fully with death and the process of dying. To do so, we need to assess how the denial of death has become commonplace in the modern world and why that is a problem. But before we turn to that analysis, we will seek to allow the saints to flip our perspective about who is really desiring whom between the living and the blessed dead.

What we hope to learn, see, and believe more deeply is something that Robert Cording, in his own grief and love for his son, already seems to know deep in his bones: he is not whole without his son. We are never whole on our own, nor are we created or called to be. In light of the promises of Christ, we long for wholeness as one people, and we become fully human together.

THE MEANING OF SALVATION

Though it is thoroughly personal, salvation is not private.

There remains in the popular imagination the indistinct idea that salvation—or heaven—is about getting out of this world and being happy beyond this world's troubles. Hidden within this idea is the assumption that it is better to be alone and happy than to be mixed up in the lives of others. The unattractiveness of such an assumption becomes noticeable immediately once you start to think about the people you love, and who love you.

Would an island paradise really be paradise if you had to leave behind those you love? If you could choose paradise, but the consequence was having your memories of your loved ones erased so that you could live in your new land untroubled, would you do it? I presume that people like Robert Cording would say, "Absolutely not!" The French novelist Jean Giono expresses the feeling this way: "My joy will not be lasting unless it is the joy of all. I will not pass through the battlefields with a rose in my hand."[4] This desire for the joy of others—which, admittedly, is often a latent desire—corresponds with the Christian understanding of the human person.

When we addressed biblical anthropology in chapter 1, we laid the foundation for the meaning of "person" in Christianity. We are created in the image of God: as God is three Persons in communion, so we are created distinct but ordered to communion with one another (see Genesis 1:26–28, 2:21–25). Communion is not sameness, and it certainly is not separateness; rather, it is the union of them who are distinct. A "person" is one who is distinct from others *and* distinctly in relationship with others; being relational is inerasable from the meaning of being a "person."[5]

To put this theological notion in concrete terms, we may say that Robert Cording is the father of Daniel Cording, and Robert is not whole without Daniel. What it means for Robert to be Robert is tied up in who and how Daniel is. Happiness for Robert is not a private island: "It is not good that the man should be alone" (Gn 2:18).

This is about more than what we may happen to want. We could certainly imagine—and may in fact know—people who really would rather be alone, or at least so it seems. But this cannot lead us to say "To each his own." Rather, Christians hold to communion as the way of life because it is the way of Christ: it is his life. Risen from the dead, he does not drift away and detach himself from this world or those whom he loves; rather, he bears the wounds of love on his glorified body and ascends to the Father with that body. The Son of God is fully human, and he is in full communion with the Father *as fully human*. His glorified body is the sign and reality of his communion with us.[6]

The body of Christ forces us to reconsider what it means for us to have bodies—to *be* bodily. It is not too much to say that you *are* your body, or more precisely, you are the *union* of your body with your soul. We might each assume we know what the body is—that material thing, the physical part of me, this . . . *stuff*. But Christ, risen bodily from the dead, demands that we broaden and deepen our notions of the body.

THE BONDS OF THE BODY

What is your body? Your body is your contact with the world; it is the space of interaction, of relationship. It is with *this* body that you feel pain, that you know joy, that you are delighted and disappointed and wounded and healed. This is the body that your mother held, that friends have embraced. Through this body you have learned all the things you know. It is this body that you and others have cared for, and that you and others have, at times, mistreated.

What is your body, then, but your history? It is the symbol, the living memory of your history, of your very presence and participation in the world with others. When we die in our bodies, all that history and presence dies with us.

Death is total, and it is humiliating. All the energy and passion, all the drama and cares and loves and fears and sufferings that we experience and undergo in this earthly life become meaningless in dead flesh. It is all for naught.

In the Resurrection of Christ, however, God returns significance to the human body. God "re-members" us, preserving all that we would lose and putting back together what has been pulled apart. The glorified body of Christ is God's pledge that our earthly lives *now* have eternal significance. What we on our own would lose, God recoups and restores and perfects.[7]

The consequences of the Christian hope in the resurrection of the body are far-reaching. In raising us in our bodies to join in communion with him, God raises our relationships, our histories, our *lives*. Who each of us is in and through our bodies is inextricably bound up in our relationships with others, through love and sin, harm and healing, kindness and callousness.

In his great love, God is attentive to us: he makes up for what is lacking in us while he blesses and perfects what is good. So it is that the hope of a father for his dead son points not just toward the raising of his son to new life but indeed toward the restoration and healing and perfection of their relationship. Salvation is never private, because human persons are made for communion. The resurrection of the body is about wholeness, absolutely.

WAITING FOR WHOLENESS

The early church father Origen of Alexandria took the social nature of salvation so seriously that he ventured to speak about Christ's own imperfect joy *now* as he waits for the perfection of the members of his full body, the Church:

> What does it mean when [Jesus] says, "I will not drink [from the fruit of this vine until I drink it with you in the Kingdom of my Father]"? My Savior grieves even now about my sins. My Savior cannot rejoice as long as I remain in perversion. Why cannot he do this? Because he himself is "an intercessor for our sins with the Father." . . . How can he, who is an intercessor for my sins, drink the "wine of joy," when I grieve him with my sins?[8]

Origen conceives of the joy of Christ as tied up in the health, well-being, and perfection of his members: those whom he loves. Christ's joy is not complete, Origen muses, because his members are not yet whole in him. Moving from this insight, Origen then considers how, by the law of charity and with abounding mercy, the members of Christ's Body wait for each other, in hope and in longing:

> For the apostles too have not yet received their joy: they likewise are waiting for me to participate in their joy. So it is that the saints who depart from here

do not immediately receive the full reward of their merits, but wait for us, even if we delay, even if we remain sluggish. They cannot know perfect joy as long as they grieve over our transgressions and weep for our sins. . . .

Do you see, then? Abraham is still waiting to attain perfection. Isaac and Jacob and all the prophets are waiting for us in order to attain the perfect blessedness together with us. This is the reason why judgment is kept a secret, being postponed until the Last Day. It is "one body" which is waiting for justification, "one body" which rises for judgment. . . .

You will have joy when you depart from this life if you are a saint. But your joy will be complete only when no member of your body is lacking to you. For you too will wait, just as you are awaited.[9]

We may feel uneasy reading Origen's words, because it sounds as if the blessed dead are being held hostage by the sins of the living. The saints cannot rest, it seems, because sinners still sin. The key to understanding Origen rightly is to recognize that all of this waiting for others is part of the love of Christ, who is himself God's saving action. The only begotten Son of God, who descended to the depths to join in solidarity with us, waits in love for us to join him as he is, where he is. The saints, who rest in Christ, join in his holy longing—they are, so to speak, safe in the sweet *unrest* of Christ, who hastens in love to attract and heal those who remain wounded by sin.

The saints are not being held hostage by sinners; they are sharing in the mercy of Christ. By his mercy, the saints long for the fullness of communion, when we will be one with them in

Christ. The fullness of communion is the completion of the resurrection of the body. The saints await this final wholeness: that is the full image of salvation, which we call the "Communion of Saints."

THE RESTLESSNESS OF LOVE

When we speak here of saints, we should also keep in view our faithful departed and think to our own death, when we will leave loved ones behind: "For you too will wait, just as you are awaited." While we may have trouble seeing how Abraham or St. Matthew bears a direct relation to us, we can more easily see that relation with those whom we have known and loved in this life.

With this mystery of holy waiting in mind and after quoting the passages from Origen that we just read, Joseph Ratzinger (Pope Benedict XVI) goes on to ask us to think seriously about the relational nature of our humanity, in very personal terms: "We can ask whether a human being can be said to have reached his fulfilment and destiny so long as others suffer on account of him, so long as the guilt whose source he is persists on earth and brings pain to other people. . . . The guilt which goes on because of me is part of me."[10] This idea may incite feelings of worry, inclining us to think about how the effect of our own sins will continue to be felt in the lives of others even after we die. We often do not see or recognize the full effect of our sins, and yet my hardness of heart becomes someone else's undue fragility, and my betrayal becomes someone else's inability to fully trust others. "I have greatly sinned, in my thoughts and in my words, in what I have done and what I have failed to do," Catholics admit in the

Confiteor, and those actions and omissions have real effects on others because our humanity is inherently social.

Ratzinger is not making a moral statement here; he is making an anthropological one. Lest we think that our social nature is a curse, we must also confess that blessings are communicated through our humanity—in and through our bodies. The fact of the matter is that God has created us in relation to one another; the question is whether we will communicate blessings or curses through our shared humanity. While sin turns our humanity into an instrument of cursing, by the grace of God and our growth in virtue, that same humanity becomes an instrument of blessing, beginning in Christ. Ratzinger therefore continues:

> It is not only the guilt we leave behind on earth that prevents our definitive reclining at table at the eschatological [or heavenly] banquet, in joy unalloyed. Whereas guilt is bondage to time, the freedom of love, conversely, is openness for time. The nature of love is always to be "for" someone. Love cannot, then, close itself against others or be without them so long as time, and with it suffering, is real. . . . In even ordinary human terms we can say, How can a mother be completely and unreservedly happy so long as one of her children is suffering?[11]

Even as a mother in life could not enjoy a holiday so long as one of her children was suffering, we might imagine that the mother, upon death, continues to concern herself with her child. It is not so much that she *cannot* rest while her child is still undergoing trial as much as that she *will not* rest. Love leads to restlessness:

loving someone means being restless for their well-being. We count the good of the other as our own.[12]

THE DESIRE OF SAINTS IN DEATH

This "anthropology of love," as we might call it, is shown to us in the mystifying words of St. Thérèse of Lisieux. In the middle of the night a couple months before she died, Thérèse sat up in bed, coughed up blood, and declared:

> I feel that I'm about to enter into my rest. But I feel especially that my mission is about to begin, my mission of making God loved as I love Him, of giving my little way to souls. If God answers my desires, my heaven will be spent on earth until the end of the world. Yes, I want to spend my heaven in doing good on earth. This isn't impossible, since from the bosom of the beatific vision, the angels watch over us. I can't make heaven a feast of rejoicing; I can't rest as long as there are souls to be saved. But when the angel will have said: "Time is no more!" then I will take my rest; I'll be able to rejoice, because the number of the elect will be complete and because all will have entered into joy and repose. My heart beats with joy at this thought.[13]

Thérèse cannot imagine a heaven where she would have to sever herself from those whom Christ called her to love. So long as Christ hastens to poor sinners in mercy, Thérèse desires to hasten toward them in *his* mercy. In her imagination, this means that until the end of time, Thérèse's heaven will be spent as a servant of Christ's mercy directed toward those still struggling on earth. She desires their well-being, and desiring their well-being is, for now, *her* joy. Salvation for Thérèse is not at all private, but it is absolutely personal.

Likewise, Teresa of Calcutta, who took Thérèse's name as her own religious name, would never dream of cutting herself off in death from the poorest of the poor whom she hastened to love throughout her life in obedience to Christ's call. She did not consider her life as a test to "get into heaven" but rather as a practice for heaven. Loving the least among us was, to Teresa, the way to learn what heaven is: the communion of all in Christ.

With a profound understanding of what it means to be genuinely human and thus of what true love is, Teresa penned words that confounded many upon their publication: "If I ever become a saint—I will surely be one of 'darkness.' I will continually be absent from heaven—to light the light to those in darkness on earth."[14] Again, how could a mother enjoy a holiday while even one of her children was suffering? For years and years, day after day, Teresa took "the unwanted, unloved, unclaimed" as her own children.[15] She loved them with a mother's fierce affection. They were a part of her: the whole Teresa includes those whom she loves. If they live in darkness, then she would choose to keep them company in the darkness rather than enjoying light all by herself (so long as Christ permitted it). Teresa chose the poor in obedience to Christ, who chooses the poor as his own beloved. Her enigmatic words and unfathomable desire give witness to Ratzinger's description of the anthropology of love: "Love cannot close itself against others or be without them as long as time, and with it suffering, is real."[16]

Saints desire in death to continue loving those whom they leave behind. The seriousness of this truth in the witness of saints like Thérèse and Teresa shocks us, forcing us to think more seriously about and imagine more boldly the love of our beloved dead for us who remain. Their longing for us may in fact exceed our longing for them.

The saints stretch across the interruption of death toward communion with us in Christ. The desire of the saints comes as a calling to the living, to respond to this desire for communion that makes a claim on us. Openness to continuing relationship—albeit on different terms—with those who have died is necessary for those of us who are "living" to be fully and wholly ourselves, as we are created and called to be. The problem, of course, is that in modern times we deny death, avoid the process of dying, and have developed the social habit of looking away from the dead as if they were not still a part of us *now* and we were not meant to be one with them in the fullness of time.

WILLFUL IGNORANCE OF DEATH

To find our beloved dead we have to look at death; ignoring death keeps the departed out of view. This sounds bizarre because we know that those who grieve are painfully aware of death's intervention. Death comes as a shock; adjusting to the change that the death of a loved one imposes on those who remain feels like an unprecedented task. And that is precisely the issue we have to address: why death has been made so foreign to us.

In modern Western culture, we willfully ignore death.[17] Turn on the television or watch a movie and there appears to be all kinds of evidence to the contrary: death is everywhere. But this is merely death made into a spectacle for entertainment, death trivialized. It is yet another way of turning our gaze from the reality of death and thus from the reality of life.

In addition to trivializing death through entertainment, Joseph Ratzinger observes, "bourgeois society hides death away" by putting it under taboo and ordering it according to "technical tasks technically handled by technical people."[18] These ways of hiding death bear significant consequences, affecting not merely our ideas or approaches to death but, indeed, what we assume it means to live. "Attitudes to dying determine attitudes to living," Ratzinger claims, before concluding: "Death becomes the key to the question: What really *is* man? The mounting callousness towards human life which we are experiencing today is intimately bound up with the refusal to confront the question of death. Repression and trivialization can only 'solve' the riddle by dissolving humanity itself."[19]

It is a strong claim to say that ignoring death dissolves our humanity, but from a Christian perspective, Ratzinger is far from indulging in hyperbole here. On the personal level, for me to refuse to reckon with the inevitability of my own death is to hide from the fact that according to my own power, my death will be a total loss. Remember what we said above about the broader and deeper meaning of the body: my body is my presence in the world among others, as well as the history of all my dramas, relationships, wounds, and growth. Death shows me that I cannot sustain myself and that I will lose everything *unless* the God who created me also raises me from the dead, in and as my body. Ratzinger is saying that I do not actually take anything in this world seriously if I do not face the fact that I will lose it all in death, with my only hope being to gain it all in Christ.

In addition to that personal sense, Ratzinger also has an *interpersonal* sense in mind, and this too is tied up with the meaning of the body and the truth of the human person. "The mounting callousness" Ratzinger points to manifests on the societal level when the suffering and death of some persons are treated as unimportant or unworthy of concern. It is as if the poor are not worthy of the concern of the rich, the sick are not worthy of the concern of the healthy, and the dying are not worthy of the concern of those who would rather get back to life as usual.

Pope Francis has at times described this callousness as a hallmark of a "throwaway culture," and in *Amoris Laetitia* he speaks of this callous disposition within relationships:

> I think too of the fears associated with permanent commitment, the obsession with free time, and those relationships that weigh costs and benefits for the sake of remedying loneliness, providing protection, or offering some service. We treat affective relationships the way we treat material objects and the environment: everything is disposable; everyone uses and throws away, takes and breaks, exploits and squeezes to the last drop. Then, goodbye. (*Amoris Laetitia*, 39; cf. *Evangelii Gaudium*, 53)

Like St. John Paul II describing the "culture of death" (see especially *Evangelium Vitae*, 12), Pope Francis describes the "throwaway culture" as ultimately reducing human beings to commodities that can be disposed of when deemed undesirable or inconvenient. The most vulnerable are the unborn and the elderly, the poor and the lowly (see, for example, *Fratelli Tutti*, 18). The main idea running through John Paul II, Ratzinger

(Benedict XVI), and then Francis is that the inherently social nature of the human person has been exchanged for a predominantly individualistic one. A culture where the "individual" reigns supreme and interpersonal relationships are, at best, secondary becomes one where we end up "using" each other rather than bearing responsibility for one another. And since taking seriously the dying and death of others is inconvenient and interrupts the pace and rhythm of what has become "normal life," dying and death are, culturally, taken out of view. The procedures for dying and the impact of death become merely "technical tasks handled technically by technical people."[20]

What is at stake in all of this is indeed what it means to be human. Am I created by God, someone whose life comes from God and goes to God, someone whose life is ultimately secured in God? And am I created with and for others, so that I am not myself by myself? When a Thérèse of Lisieux or Teresa of Calcutta desires to be united to lowly, lonely, and forgotten persons even in their deaths, they protest against the reduction of humanity to a collection of separate individuals. When someone mourning the death of a loved one feels suddenly out of place in a world that keeps rushing along as if nothing at all has changed, it is an indication not that the mourner is deranged, or that other people are selfish or blind, but rather that the broader culture is sick in its treatment of death as an aberration and of the dead as unproductive and therefore unimportant.

This has not always been the case; in fact, it is only in the past century that such attitudes toward death and dying have become commonplace. Over the past thousand years, there has been a slow, centuries-long drift away from a more communal approach to dying and death that has then rapidly accelerated in the span of several decades. The result of this slow-then-rapid shift is a radically individualized approach to both life and death.

SHIFTING WESTERN APPROACHES TO DEATH AND DYING

The French medievalist and social historian Philippe Ariès specialized in the study of death and dying—or rather, the study of people's attitudes toward death and dying. His comprehensive work *The Hour of Our Death* meticulously traces the at first slowly changing attitudes toward death over the past millennium before showing how these attitudes rapidly morphed in the last century. Ariès begins his study in the Middle Ages and there finds what had been the norm in approaches to death for centuries prior; this is also the norm against which he measures the changes in the approach to death over the subsequent ten centuries. In short, he finds that death was treated as a natural and important part of life.[21]

In what we might call the "classic approach," common for most of the previous millennium, people were familiar with the death of others and with their own death. A good death was considered one that a person could prepare for, meaning that they knew they were going to die and could thus be active and engaged throughout the process of dying. Death usually took place in the home, in the company of family members (including children) and members of the community. There were well-established customs surrounding the process of dying and the period after death. It was of course a single person who was dying and then died, but this death was also a communal affair. There was no attempt to separate an "individual" from the community; quite to the contrary, the entire community was involved in the death of a single person. Death was a pain borne together.

The slow change in the "classic approach" to death transpired between the late eleventh and mid-fifteenth centuries. From studying art, literature, and social customs, Ariès shows that the focus began to trend slightly more toward the individual and away from what was previously a primary concern: the collective destiny of all humankind (put another way, the social nature of salvation). This change in focus signaled the first shift.

Evidence of a second shift appeared in artistic renderings of judgment, where the scene for judgment is no longer at the end of the world but in the bedchamber of the dying individual. In other words, the time of judgment is pinned to the moment of death, not the end of time, which calls into question the social nature of humanity and the broader meaning of the human body.

This shift was joined by a third one—the sudden appearance of cadavers in art—which further emphasized the move in attention toward the individual, and with this move grew a looming sense of anxiety for the hour of death. Ariès summarizes the effect of these slow-developing shifts: "Beginning with the eleventh century, a formerly unknown relationship developed between the death of each individual and his awareness of being an individual. . . . In the mirror of his own death each man would discover the secret of his individuality."[22] These shifts in the late medieval period were significant because they marked the start of a longer process of separating individuals from their communities in social, religious, artistic, and literary contexts. In short, the "classic approach" was beginning to fray.

In the Romantic era (roughly the eighteenth and nineteenth centuries), the sensitivity to the separation of individuals from one another found a new expression and a new form of anxiety when the death of the "other" captured popular attention. Death was shown to be greedy and aggressive, taking what it wanted and making the dead disappear. Loved ones were snatched away by death, disturbing and interrupting the "ordinary life" of the living. Whereas death had long been familiar within families, communities, and households, "a new intolerance of separation"[23] on the part of survivors took hold, as they no longer approached death through the language of longstanding customs. "Death has become something metaphysical," Ariès comments regarding this change throughout the Romantic era. It was now seen to be "like the separation of man and wife or two dear friends. . . . The pain of death [was] seen not as the real suffering of the death agony but as something comparable to the sorrow of a broken friendship."[24]

When death is viewed as a definitive break, as loss, and strictly as sorrow, death is then to be resisted and avoided at all cost. The old customs of the "classic approach" facilitated communication between the dying person and his circumstances, the person and his community, and the living and the dead, but these customs no longer serve if the new aim is to turn away from death and the separation it imposes. New customs are called for—customs that hide circumstances from the dying person, hide the dying person from the outside world, hide the sufferings of grief and mourning from "normal life," and hide dying and death behind professional services.

Whereas the familiarity with death that the old customs guarded endured for centuries, Ariès claims that "the complete reversal in customs seems to have occurred in one generation."[25] That generation spanned the late nineteenth to the mid-twentieth centuries, when society's aim became to make death invisible. The invisibility of death, which goes hand in hand with the separation of individuals from one another, is the defining characteristic of what we might call the "modern approach."

Three new, radical shifts signaled the advent of the "modern approach," which quickly took precedence. First, new customs were introduced to keep the dying person ignorant about their own fate and circumstances. The motive here was likely a kind of compassion: since death had come to be viewed primarily as separation and demise, people tried to save the dying person from having to face the unpleasantness of his situation. Euphemistic speech was introduced, hopes for survival against all odds were recited, and plans for continued living were rehearsed. Whereas previously a desirable death was one for which a person could prepare, now the acceptable style of death was one where the dying person pretended they were not going to die.[26]

The second shift in customs in the new, "modern approach" to dying and death emerged most clearly around the time of World War I. This shift concerned the "taboo against mourning and everything in public life that reminded one of death, at least the so-called natural (i.e., nonviolent) death."[27] In a time when great suffering on the world stage became unavoidably present, those who mourned publicly were like potential superspreaders of a dreaded virus: they were liable to spread the contagion to others, or at least bother others with their malady. Ariès therefore claims that the new societal approach to mourners could be likened to quarantining those with contagious diseases: they had to be cordoned off until the sickness was inoculated. Mourning was now to be as brief and private as possible.[28]

The third and final shift in the "modern approach" to death was the most important of all: Ariès calls it the "medicalization of death." This shift entailed a broad array of changes in modern life relative to death, but the main change was the relocation of the sick and dying from the home to the hospital. In this contained environment, experts and specialists could preside over the dying process.[29] The dying and dead were kept out of contact with the ordinary happenings of the world, as they are granted a secluded place for suffering that also allows for the security of "collective happiness."[30]

Ariès says this "modern approach" to death seeks the "forbidden death" and the "invisible death."[31] This new set of social practices, which are common for us today but would have been distinctly uncommon for people living in the thousand years before us, establishes a culture where death can be either forgotten or "domesticated once and for all by the advance of technology, especially medical technology."[32] Though individuals feel the loss of their loved ones, the community as a whole is protected from feeling too grievously the death of any of its members. This is a form of social self-preservation, which in the end, Ariès says, is indicative of the modern world. Undertaker and essayist Thomas Lynch argues that this erasure of death from communal life leads to the general "inability to deal authentically with life."[33]

This movement from the "classic approach" to the "modern approach" to dying and death is a cultural phenomenon that has shifted what is considered normal.[34] Whereas for centuries it was normal in the Western world to bear with dying and deal with death in communal settings, in the modern world it is normal to keep death out of the public eye (except for entertainment purposes) so that dying is a predominantly individual event. It is therefore in concert with Ratzinger (Benedict XVI) and Francis and John Paul II that Ariès declares that this modern world "no longer has a sufficient sense of solidarity; it has actually abandoned responsibility for the organization of collective life. The community in the traditional sense of the word no longer exists. It has been replaced by an enormous mass of atomized individuals."[35]

THE HEALTHY SHOCK OF GRIEF

The grief that people feel over the death of their loved ones is healthy. In fact, this grief can be an awakening to the urgent reminder of a truth that has been largely neglected in the modern world. Mourning the death of loved ones reveals to us that we are not, in fact, "atomized individuals." The lack of wholeness that Robert Cording experienced after his son's death was a painful and truthful reminder that we are not ourselves by ourselves.

"Where are you?" Robert's wife cried into the darkness over and over again the night their son Daniel died. "We cannot imagine our loved ones are nowhere," Robert wrote later. "Or perhaps," he continued, "the question is simply 'Are you?' since it is oblivion, not location, we fear."[36]

As the raw grief of the first night of a loved one's death becomes the settled grief of the months and years to follow, the truly human response is not to "get over" the sense of incompleteness that the death of a loved one imposes. Rather, the truly human response is to keep reaching out, keep longing for, keep crying "Where are you?" to the ones without whom we will never be whole. The hole is not meant to be filled until we are united in that "world of love" that Jonathan Edwards preached on. Until then, the duty of those who remain is to live as if the dead are in communion with us in this life, in this world, *now.*

The pastor, theologian, and martyr Dietrich Bonhoeffer spoke of this duty in letters to his loved ones while imprisoned and awaiting trial (and eventual execution) at the hands of the Nazis. On Christmas Eve, 1943, he wrote a letter about what is most important in times of separation:

> First: nothing can make up for the absence of someone whom you love, and it would be wrong to try to find a substitute; we must simply hold out and see it through. That sounds very hard at first, but at the same time it is a great consolation, for the gap, as long as it remains unfilled, preserves the bond between us. It is nonsense to say that God fills the gap; he doesn't fill it, but on the contrary, he keeps it empty and so helps us to keep alive our former communion with each other, even at the cost of pain.
>
> Second: the dearer and richer our memories, the more difficult the separation. But gratitude changes the pangs of memory into a tranquil joy. . . . We must take care not to wallow in our memories . . . [but keep them] as a hidden treasure that is ours for certain. . . .
>
> Third: times of separation are not a total loss . . . they can be the means of strengthening fellowship quite remarkably.
>
> Fourthly: . . . From the moment we wake until we fall asleep we must commend other people wholly and unreservedly to God and leave them in his hands.[37]

The gap, Bonhoeffer says, points to the bond between those who are separated. That gap is not just sorrow; when memories of former communion and hope for future communion are added to it, the gap can become an occasion for gratitude, for being united to one another. The time of separation is itself the occasion for increasing the desire for union, but above all the duty of those who are separated is to commend each other into the hands of God. This response to the separation from loved ones—especially in death—does not deny the separation, does not sink into despair at the separation, and does not fail to continue to seek union "even at the cost of pain." Above all, this response arises from a Christian view of the human person, who is never strictly an isolated individual but is irreducibly relational and only whole in communion with others.

The truly urgent task for fostering communion with the dead is not just to strengthen our good intentions but indeed to develop practices for communion. This means rebuilding a culture of communion, where especially those who mourn discover that they are not alone in their grief because a community bears the loss with them. If the new customs of the "modern approach" to death isolate individuals from one another, then other customs must be either recovered or established to return the experiences of dying and of death to communal life.

It is toward this renewal of life in communion that we now begin to move in the latter portions of this book, motivated by the firm conviction that *we* become fully human together.

We: the living and the dead.

4.

SACRED MEMORY AND THE WORK OF MERCY

As a teenager, John Cavadini took the bus to school. Picked up early in the route, he sat in the front and saved the seat next to him for a boy who got picked up later. Nobody liked that boy. John saved a seat for him because he knew that if this boy had to sit in the back of the bus, his entire ride to school would be one long merciless affair of others making fun of him. At the end of high school, the boy wrote in John's yearbook, "Thanks for sitting with me on the bus."

Some five decades later, John learned that that boy, now of course a man, had died in a treatment center, alone, with nobody to care for him. This person was not dear to John, but he was someone who might otherwise be forgotten. So John chose to let that now-dead man matter to him: "That guy, who was alone in life, was alone in death, and probably not in great circumstances. Wouldn't you want him to be surprised that someone actually does love him more than sitting with him on the bus, sort of grudgingly? So he's on my list; I pray for him all the time. I even told one of my kids about him, and he had a Mass said for him."[1]

The idea of keeping a list of dead people to pray for was something John learned from Dorothy Day. She kept her list of

79

the dead in her prayer book, and every day she would go through it during her prayers and offer a prayer for the dead whom she had claimed. As she got older, her list got longer and longer, and it took more and more of her time to pray for all the people. Her list included people she had known well, people she had known only a little, and people who had no one else to pray for them. Dorothy made it a practice to include the dead in her daily routine, and John took on Dorothy's practice as his own. The boy from the bus who died as a man alone in a treatment center is now remembered in John's personal prayer and through the sacrifice of the Mass.[2]

Those who pray for the dead make space in their lives for those who no longer have any space of their own and cannot help themselves. They are helpless and, in natural terms, useless to the living. They cannot do anything concrete for us. To pray for those who have died is to heed poverty and respond with generosity.

And yet is not the one who prays also somehow changed by the dead for whom they pray? The absence of the person who might otherwise be forgotten becomes, through prayer, a sort of presence. That person whom you remember becomes present to you in your mind and heart, in time and circumstance, here and now. Even the briefest prayer gives the dead person a part of you: some parcel of memory, some span of attention, some movement of will. The act of praying for the dead makes it so that *the one who prays* is not alone. Prayer is protest against isolation, a declaration of communion.

There are no grand acts for exercising communion between the living and the dead, and at the same time they are all grand acts. The revolution of what is considered normal is at stake. We are either created as one and called to communion, or we are not. The way in which we who are living remember and seek communion with our dead makes manifest our belief in the promises of Christ.

"Praying for the dead is a work of mercy," John Cavadini says. "All the works of mercy are acts which treat someone as an end in themselves and not as something to be used for another goal or end."[3] A throwaway culture measures people on their usefulness and values them according to what they can do for you. A culture of mercy values people as God's beloved creatures, claimed and redeemed in Christ.

Building a culture of mercy requires more than the sporadic actions of individuals. Cultures are built through habitual practices and customs that become more and more common to the people who share life together. People like Dorothy Day are innovators of culture through what they themselves do and what they teach other people to do. John Cavadini joined the culture Dorothy helped promote, a culture in which the living join themselves to the dead in prayer.

In seeking to better understand the communion between the living and the dead, we must not only explore but reimagine and recommit to the habitual practices that build a culture of mercy. For Christians, the truly human, truly merciful culture always begins in and grows from the mercy of Christ. In this chapter, then, we will begin with St. Augustine to learn anew how Christ's gift of himself in the Eucharist creates the space for mercy between the living and the dead. From that vantage point, we will be able to learn from the cultural exercises of communion with the dead manifested in devotions and pious traditions before contemplating the necessarily social meaning of purgatory.

FOUR DEATHS AND A SOLEMN OFFERING

The narrative of St. Augustine's conversion includes a dramatic shift in his approach to death and grieving. The first encounter with the death of a loved one that he recounts concerns the death of a friend whom he describes as "exceedingly dear to me."[4] The death of another dear friend, the death of his son, and the death of his mother follow. It is with the death of his mother—who was most dear to him—that the transformation of his approach to death nears completion in a Eucharistic offering.

When Augustine was a young man, he enjoyed a very close friendship with a peer who shared many of Augustine's own interests. For a year, they were inseparable. Then his friend became severely ill and was baptized while unconscious. Augustine thought Baptism ridiculous and so, expecting his friend to think the same, went to him when he awoke and started to make fun of the sacrament. To Augustine's surprise, his friend rebuked him. Augustine was intent on trying to lure his friend back to his own way of thinking, but his friend's health quickly declined, and he died while Augustine "was not there."[5]

If you look through Augustine's account of his friendship with this young man, one very important detail is missing: the friend's name. This is part of Augustine's point. At that time in his life, Augustine did not cherish this friend as a person unto himself but strictly as "my friend." In other words, though unknowingly at the time, Augustine made this young man into what he, Augustine, wanted him to be. This is why Augustine was so surprised and bothered when his friend rebuffed Augustine's attempts to ridicule his baptism. Suddenly, this young man was not fitting the script Augustine was writing for him.

Upon his friend's death, Augustine writes, "Black grief closed over my heart and wherever I looked I saw only death."[6] Augustine is not mourning for his friend but rather for himself. He grieves over what he, Augustine, has lost: "My eyes sought him everywhere, but he was missing; I hated all things because they held him not."[7] Augustine wants his friend to remain forever what Augustine wanted him to be. Now that his friend is gone, Augustine grieves what he no longer has. This black grief is a grief that does not go anywhere. There is nothing for Augustine to do with it: it closes over him and everything is loss.

It is important to keep this unnamed friend in mind when we come across Augustine's account of the death of another dear friend later in life, after Augustine himself had received Baptism and entered the Church. This friend also became Christian and brought his entire household into the Church with him. When he dies, this friend has been living a Christian life, just as Augustine is striving to do. In his address to God, Augustine says of his friend, "And now he lives in Abraham's bosom. Whatever that may be, whatever the gospel word 'bosom' may mean, there my Nebridius is living, to me a friend most tenderly loved, to you, Lord, a freedman adopted as your son; yes, there he lives on."[8]

This friend is no less dear to him than the previous one, but Augustine holds this friendship very differently. First, we cannot help but notice that whereas the other friend was reduced to being Augustine's nameless appendage, *this* friend has a name: Nebridius. Second, though Augustine claims Nebridius in friendship, he recognizes that he does not own him. Instead, he confesses that Nebridius is an adopted son of God (by virtue of his baptism), and this identity contextualizes his identity as Augustine's friend. Third and finally, Augustine proclaims Nebridius as living in God. He does not know fully what that means, but he trusts that what Christ has said about the dead who live in him is true. With his previous, unnamed friend, there was only death—namely, the black grief that Augustine felt at the friend's absence. With Nebridius, he offers his friend in faith to God, who gives life. The way in which he speaks of the death of Nebridius marks a major shift in Augustine's approach to death.

Augustine provides further testimony to this transformed approach to death when he speaks of the death of someone else very close to him: his son, Adeodatus. Augustine fathered this boy while he was living with a woman out of wedlock, before his conversion. He says, therefore, that the boy was "born of my sin."[9] He goes on and on, praising the virtues of this young man, lauding his intelligence and his fairness. As he does so, Augustine is keen to confess that he himself can take no credit for this young man's goodness, attributing these blessings instead to God his creator. "Nothing did I contribute to that boy's making but my own fault," Augustine says; "it was you [O Lord], and you alone, who had inspired us to instruct him in your truth as he grew up, and so it is your own gifts that I acknowledge to you."[10] Attributing the wonder of his own son to the goodness of the Lord frees Augustine to entrust his son to the love of the Lord upon the boy's untimely death. "I remember him without anxiety," Augustine confesses, "for I have no fear about anything in his boyhood or adolescence; indeed I fear nothing whatever for that man."[11] In learning to see his son as a gift from God in life, Augustine is able to confidently offer his son to God in death.

It is with the death of his mother, Monica, however, that Augustine experiences the deepest grief and, ultimately, the greatest act of sacrifice. As he begins to detail what he experienced upon his mother's death, Augustine says that his grief was very deep and that he even grieved over just how deep his grief was: "The woe I felt over my woe was yet another woe."[12] Rather than settling into his despair and allowing grief to close over him, Augustine does something he did not do when he grieved so deeply over his unnamed friend: he begs God to heal his pain.[13]

Occupied as Augustine is with his own pain, though, he opens himself to caring about his mother rather than only focusing on what he himself has lost: "I pour out to you tears [O Lord] . . . for this servant of yours."[14] His prayers for his mother redound to a plea for her healing—specifically, the healing of her sins, even though Augustine considers her the most charitable and grace-filled person he knew.[15] Augustine begs God in tears for his mother's well-being.

For a man who long suffered from commitment issues and an unwillingness to sacrifice, these tears signify a substantial conversion of heart and will. In heeding his mother's own need and praying for her well-being, Augustine remains obedient to his mother, who wept for him and prayed for his conversion over many long years. In that obedience, he recalls Monica's own requests for how he, Augustine, should remember her: "She desired only to be remembered at your altar where she had served you every day."[16]

Monica, who devoted her life to serving the Lord and drew near to the sacrifice of the Eucharist, instructed her son to offer his own prayers for her to the Lord in the Eucharist. This is what Augustine does. With tears and longing, on his knees, Augustine approaches the Eucharistic Lord and begs him to remember his mother—to draw her in death to himself, who is life. As a final, prodigal act of love, Augustine then turns to his readers and asks *us* to join him in offering our prayers to the Eucharistic Lord on her behalf: "So may the last request she made of me be granted her more abundantly by the prayer of many, evoked by my confessions, than by my prayers alone."[17]

From the death of his unnamed friend to the death of his friend Nebridius, Augustine learns to let go of his control over those dear to him and to see them above all as God's beloved. With his son, Adeodatus, he practices giving thanks to God for this young man's goodness in life and so finds the confidence to entrust the boy to the Lord's goodness in death. With his mother, Monica, Augustine finally lives into the full Christian response to the death of a loved one. In tears, he commits himself not only to prayer but especially to offering his prayers at the altar of the Lord. It is upon that altar, where the Lord gives himself in the Eucharist, that Augustine beckons others to join him in forging communion with his mother in the love of Christ.

THE EUCHARISTIC PRAYER

Monica directed her son to bring his prayers for her to the altar. Sixteen centuries later, John Cavadini's son carried his father's prayers for his erstwhile classmate to the altar. On the altar where the Lord's gift of himself in the Eucharist meets his people, those prayers for the dead find a new beginning.

What happens at the Eucharist? Christ gives his Body and Blood to his Church. Those who receive, receive him. The communion of Christ himself opens wide. Offering prayers for the dead at the sacrifice of the altar means begging the Lord to take the dead into his communion. Those who receive the Sacrament of Communion in the Eucharistic bread and wine are beckoned into the communion of all Christ's members. This entire ineffable mystery is made verbal in the Eucharistic Prayers of the liturgy—most notably in the Roman Canon (i.e., Eucharistic Prayer I). The same mystery is presented through the other Eucharistic Prayers, too, but listening closely to the prayer of the Roman Canon—and perhaps also visualizing it—can help us recognize what exactly Christ gives when he gives himself in the Blessed Sacrament.

At the beginning of the Liturgy of the Eucharist, the faithful bring the gifts of bread and wine to the altar; at the end, the faithful receive the Body and Blood of Christ under the appearance of that same bread and wine. In between, the Church prays that the Lord will receive these gifts and make them, for us, the Eucharistic gift that only the Lord himself can give. It is the Lord's action that is decisive, and the Church prays in faith that the Lord will indeed act as he promises he will.

The Eucharistic Prayer stretches across the dialogue between the Church who prays and the Lord who acts. In the center of that prayer are the words of institution, in which the Church invokes the *anamnesis*—or sacred memory—of Christ, as the priest makes Christ's own voice present in saying, "Take this, all of you, and eat of it, for this is my body, which will be given up for you. . . . Take this, all of you, and drink from it, for this is the chalice of my blood, the blood of the new and eternal covenant, which will be poured out for you and for many for the forgiveness of sins. Do this in memory of me."[18]

If we were to visualize the Eucharistic Prayer on a horizontal plane moving from left to right, the words of Christ in this sacred memory would appear directly in the middle. To the left of Christ's own words, we would find the names of a company of saints arranged in a very particular order: "In communion with those whose memory we venerate, especially the glorious ever-Virgin Mary," followed by her spouse and a company of "blessed Apostles and Martyrs."[19] On the opposite side of Christ's own words—that is, to the right on our horizontal plane—we would find yet another company of saints with whom the Church at prayer asks to be united. In this company, John the Baptist leads fourteen named martyrs "and all your Saints."[20]

In the Eucharistic Prayer, then, we see—or hear—how the Church proclaims in her prayer the Communion of Saints that is drawn into the sacred memory of Jesus Christ. Seeing the whole thing, we begin to grasp what the Sacrament of Communion signifies and makes present: Christ in the center, with his saints on either side. But this sacrament is no static image of Christ surrounded by his saints. At the beginning, before the company led by the Blessed Mother is named, the Church at prayer asks the Lord to remember his servants for whom the Mass is offered "and all gathered here."[21] Anticipating the sacred memory of Christ that is about to be invoked, the Church asks that those who gather for this sacrament be included in the gift of communion they shall receive. Then, once again, near the end, just before John the Baptist and his company are named, the priest says, "To us also, your servants, who, though sinners, hope in your abundant mercies, graciously grant some share and fellowship with your holy Apostles and Martyrs."[22] In the very same extended prayer whereby the faithful recognize Christ gathering to himself the glorious saints, the faithful also beg that, through the gift of the sacrament, they will be gathered into that holy company with Christ.

Holy Communion is the sacrament joining the saints in glory to the faithful, who, though sinners, approach the altar to receive the Body and Blood of Christ. And yet the communion that is offered and asked for is deeper and thicker still. Just to the right of Christ's sacred words and before the company of John the Baptist, the Church asks the Lord to perform another act of memory: "Remember also, Lord, your servants (N.) and (N.), who have gone before us with the sign of faith and rest in the sleep of peace. Grant them, O Lord, we pray, and all who sleep in Christ, a place of refreshment, light and peace. Through Christ our Lord. Amen."[23] This petition proclaims the Eucharist as a prayer for the dead. Approaching the Eucharist, the Church begs that the dead join the living faithful in the Communion of Saints, held together as one in the Body and Blood of Christ. This prayer is not only *offered up* from this altar; this prayer also *receives a response* from the altar. As he did for Thomas the Apostle, the Lord approaches communicants so that we may touch him in his Body and his Blood. He gives us himself as the pledge and guarantee of the communion we ask for. We encounter him. This is the fullness of Christ's gift to us in the Eucharist: he gives himself as he is in communion with his Father, as he is in communion with those who live in him. In each Eucharist, we who gather participate in the Lord's communion and await that communion's completion in the fullness of time.

The Eucharist is not the end of prayer; it is rather the beginning of a new culture of communion. Outside the tomb, the Lord told Mary of Magdala not to hold on to him for he had not yet ascended to the Father. In the Eucharist, Christ comes to his people to draw us into the fullness of communion: we are to ascend with him, in him. We are to seek in him not only the glorious saints but also our beloved dead. Christ comes to us as we are so that we may join him where he is.[24]

When Monica directed her son to remember her at the altar of the Lord, she sent him to the One who would make them both whole in his joy and bring them together by his Body and his Blood. When John Cavadini's son carried the petition for the man who died alone in a treatment center to the sacrifice of the Mass, he brought forward a gift of prayer that the Lord might bless and return in the Sacrament of Communion. Under the appearance of bread and wine, the eyes of faith discern the Body and Blood of Christ, the saints he holds to himself in communion, and the dead he remembers in his mercy.

THE PRAYER OVER THE OFFERINGS

When a Mass is offered for those who have died, the prayer for the dead is part of the offering the faithful bring to the altar. Augustine offered his prayer for his mother, Monica, just as the prayer for John's former classmate was offered along with the bread and wine. During Eucharistic liturgies dedicated specifically for the dead, what the Church prays for is discernible in the prayer over the offerings—that is, the prayer said over the bread and wine before consecration. By more closely attending to these prayers, we can better sense what we confess in faith regarding the communion between the living and the dead through the Eucharist.

On the day when the Church reveres the glory of all the saints and especially the anonymous saints—the Solemnity of All Saints—the Church prays this prayer over the offerings: "May these offerings we bring in honor of all the Saints be pleasing to you, O Lord, and grant that, just as we believe the Saints to be already assured of immortality, so we may experience their concern for our salvation. Through Christ Our Lord."[25] In this one prayer the Church makes a concession and a request. She concedes that there is no need to harbor concern for those celebrated in this Mass—both those whose names are known and the anonymous saints—for they already share in the eternal glory of God. The request, therefore, is not for them but for ourselves: that we may "experience *their* concern for our salvation." Celebrating the saints means celebrating those who concern themselves with our good. We might imagine Thérèse of Lisieux or Teresa of Calcutta concerning themselves with the well-being of those whom they have loved in this life, whom they continue to seek in Christ's mercy. They pray for us, and we pray that their prayers may be fruitful.

On the next day, All Souls' Day—when the Church commemorates all the faithful departed—the Church's prayer over the offerings changes: "Look favorably on our offerings, O Lord, so that your departed servants may be taken up into glory with your Son, in whose great mystery of love we are all united. Who lives and reigns for ever and ever."[26] This prayer is offered for those about whom we do still exercise concern. It is a prayer of commendation: we entrust to the mercy of God those whom we have no power to help on our own. To ask the Lord to take our loved ones into that "great mystery of love [in whom] we are all united" is to ask not only that those we love may be filled with new life but also that that life may be filled with concern for our own salvation. For the faithful departed to share in the glory the saints enjoy, they must come to fully desire what the saints desire: the salvation of others, including ourselves. In this sense, we who offer this Mass beg that, in his mercy, the Lord may make the faithful departed hasten in mercy toward *us* who now pray.

We can hear something similar in the prayer over the offerings at two Masses offered for particular loved ones who have died. First, at a funeral outside Easter time, the Church prays over the offerings in this way: "Be near, O Lord, we pray, to your servant (N.), on whose funeral day we offer you this sacrifice of conciliation, so that, should any stain of sin have clung to him (her) or any human fault have affected him (her), it may, by your loving gift, be forgiven and wiped away. Through Christ our Lord."[27] The small sacrifice of bread and wine that the faithful present upon the altar is taken up into the tremendous sacrifice of Christ's own Body and Blood, given for us. This is the "sacrifice of conciliation," through which those who are separated from God by sin are reconciled to God by the love of the Son. In a similar way, the faithful bring their prayers for their departed loved one to the altar in hope that he or she will be joined to Christ in his mercy. The small sacrifice of prayer meets the tremendous sacrifice of Christ's death. Those gathered in prayer have no power to bring back together what death has separated—all they can do is offer their need and their desire to the One who took on our death and rose again on the third day. This one humble, magnificent act of the believing community commends the deceased loved one to the Lord's care. In doing so, the community asks that "any stain of sin" or "human fault" be forgiven and wiped away. These stains and faults are all ways of failing to entrust ourselves into God's hands, and they include the ways we have harmed one another.[28] When the Church prays for this healing, she prays that the one who has died be healed of their lack of trust and charity, and that the members who commend this person also be healed of their failures to live together in communion. In this liturgy, the faithful pray that the lack of love in which the separated member and those still living have indulged may be healed and transformed into mutual concern for one another.

The second occasion when a Mass is offered for a particular loved one is on the anniversary of death. Over the offerings on this day, the Church prays with these words: "Look with favor, we pray, O Lord, on the offerings we make for the soul of your servant (N.), that, being cleansed by heavenly remedies, his (her) soul may be ever alive and blessed in your glory. Through Christ our Lord."[29] The "heavenly remedies" mentioned here deserve special consideration. Weren't these heavenly remedies administered to the disciples who encountered Jesus in the forty days after his Resurrection and before his Ascension? Didn't Laura Kelly Fanucci feel something of these remedies when she experienced unbroken joy while holding her dying daughter? Aren't these what Jonathan Edwards led his congregation to imagine and long for when he preached on heaven as a world of love? The heavenly remedies cure us, completing in us what we lack now in full: impassibility, subtlety, agility, and clarity—the properties of glorified bodies. In the small offering the living make, we ask the Lord to make our departed loved ones fit to share in his glory, just as he began to transform his disciples when he encountered them in the light of the Resurrection. We pray that *Christ's* glory will become *their* glory, so that they may become as he is. This prayer, in line with the other prayers over the offerings that have come before it, is a prayer for the wholeness, wellness, and perfection of the departed loved one, whose perfection will make them capable of perfect communion with us in Christ. The "heavenly remedies" we ask the Lord to bestow upon them will also need to be bestowed upon us who remain, so that together we may be well and whole.

These prayers over the offerings school us in what to pray for and what to desire for our beloved dead. Just as we who bring forth the bread and wine have no power on our own to make these humble gifts into the Body and Blood of Christ, so too do we who pray for our dead lack the power to raise them to new life and join them in everlasting communion. Only the Lord can give his Body and his Blood with the bread and the wine, and only he can give the communion we need and desire. It is the responsibility of those who remain to ask. Seeking communion with our loved ones in the Lord is itself the beginning of the communion we seek, because the Lord is faithful and gives what he promises.[30]

POPULAR PIETY AND THE EUCHARIST

The Eucharist is "the source and summit of the whole Christian life" (*Lumen Gentium*, 11; cf. *CCC*, 1324). The Christian life may thus be understood as a pilgrimage from grace to grace—departing from the encounter with the Lord and journeying toward the encounter with the Lord. In the fullness of time, that pilgrimage is complete when God is all in all, and the Communion of Saints is whole. The encounter with the Lord is the beginning, the end, and the fulfillment of the Christian life.

Far from canceling out popular and pious religious devotions, the encounter with the Lord in the Eucharist renews the vibrancy of such devotions and gives them their ultimate meaning. As the Second Vatican Council's *Sacrosanctum Concilium* (Constitution on the Sacred Liturgy) instructs: "The Christian people's devotions, provided they conform to the laws and norms of the Church, are to be highly recommended. . . . [S]uch devotions should be so drawn up that they harmonize with the liturgical seasons, accord with the sacred liturgy, are in some way derived from it, and lead the people to it, since in fact the liturgy by its very nature is far superior to any of them" (13).

The liturgy does not exhaust Christian spirituality but rather informs and uplifts authentically Christian spiritual customs and practices. These customs and practices vivify the "life" of which the Eucharist is "source and summit." In other words, there is an actual life in between each Eucharistic liturgy. It is that life that emerges from the end of the Mass, and it is that life that is included in the offerings carried up to the altar for consecration.

When Monica instructed her son Augustine to unite his prayers for her to the Eucharistic offering, she passed along a practice she herself had learned. For years and years while living in North Africa, Monica practiced a custom drawn from the traditional cult of the ancestors common to the peoples of that region. She followed this custom not as a pagan but as a Christian, meaning that when she brought pottage, bread, and wine to the tombs of the martyrs, she did so as a way of remembering and praying for the beloved dead. Others who followed this custom often did so in large part to indulge heavily in the wine themselves, which made the custom, in its more pagan form, something of an excuse for drunkenness. But when Monica followed Augustine to Milan and thus came under the tutelage of the local bishop, Ambrose, he instructed her to amend her former practice precisely because it was commonly associated with those irreverent indulgences.

Because Monica trusted Ambrose and his teaching so much, she willingly changed her long-held practice of bringing tokens to the tombs of the dead. She did not, however, give up her desire to remember and pray for the dead; instead, as Augustine recalls, "she had now seen the wisdom of bringing to the martyrs' shrines not a basket full of the fruits of the earth, but a heart full of more purified offerings, her prayers. In consequence she was now able to give alms to the needy [with the goods she previously reserved for the dead], and it was also possible for the sacrament of the Lord's Body to be celebrated at these shrines."[31]

The interaction between Ambrose and Monica here is an example of what *Sacrosanctum Concilium* teaches: the people's devotions are to be highly encouraged, but they must also be chastened by and directed to the Eucharistic offering. From the customs of her people, Monica brought forth a committed concern for the beloved dead. Ambrose then taught Monica how to amend her practice for a more fitting expression of the Christian faith, without in any way dampening her piety. In fact, Ambrose sought to enflame Monica's piety by ordering it to the Lord's own sacrificial offering and almsgiving.

The faith of Monica is needed now more than ever. Hers was a faith that was passionate, humble, and persuasive. She exercised concern for the dead with genuine passion, she humbly adapted her practices to the instruction of legitimate and understanding ecclesiastical authority, and she formed her son in her customs, which he then passed on to countless others. Where are the Monicas of today—the ones who oppose a culture of individualism and initiate a culture of communion, especially communion with the dead? Monica, a Catholic layperson, brought the strong devotion to the beloved dead north from Africa to the Church in Milan in the fourth century; today, for the Church in the United States, it may well be that the renewal of the devotion to the dead comes north from Mexico.

THE DAY OF THE DEAD AND CULTURAL RENEWAL

The popular religious celebration Día de los Muertos (the Day of the Dead) is founded upon and expresses a view of life (and death) that is at odds with what has become common in "modern," post-Enlightenment cultures.[32] The underlying view in Día de los Muertos is "an understanding of death not as the opposite of life but as an intrinsic part of life," so that "the enemy of life is not death but *individual* life . . . isolation from loving relationships."[33] The theologian Roberto Goizueta goes so far as to say that "what, for dominant U.S. culture, is the human ideal ('the rugged individualism') is, for Mexican Americans, the most *in*human form of existence."[34] Día de los Muertos is not, therefore, a singular event of remembrance but rather an expression of an entire approach to life—one based first on relationship rather than on individualism.

When the Spanish first brought Catholicism to central Mexico in the sixteenth century, the Christians and the Indigenous peoples kept some customs that resembled each other. Along with honoring the dead through All Saints' Day, All Souls' Day, and Masses offered for the dead, Spanish Catholics also honored the dead in their homes and in cemeteries. Moreover, bread prepared for All Souls' Day was offered as alms to the poor: "Communion between the living and the dead took the form of mutual assistance."[35]

And yet "the ritual importance of honoring the dead was far greater in Indigenous than in Catholic practice."[36] The Indigenous peoples engaged in long periods of preparation to honor their dead so that particular occasions for such honor were preceded by seasons of concerted attention and planning. Living in relationship with the dead was common to life overall rather than a facet of occasional observance. This approach to honoring the dead and the ethos that underlies it are still clearly evident in places like Oaxaca, Mexico, where Día de los Muertos thrives. In such places, death is viewed not as the end of life and the point of severance of the dead from the living but rather as a change in the circumstances of those who live together in relationship.[37]

The energy to honor the dead and the holistic investment in living in communion with the dead now contrasts sharply with the drift toward "atomized individualism" that Philippe Ariès detects in his historical study of approaches to death and dying.[38] This approach is also at odds with the "fear of permanent commitment" that Pope Francis bemoans (*Amoris Laetitia*, 53), as well as with "the mounting callousness" toward others that Joseph Ratzinger (Pope Benedict XVI) decries.[39] It is not a Christian culture that opposes the energy for and commitment to communion with the dead; rather, it is a consumer culture that stands in opposition. The dominant culture in places like the United States is often a consumer culture that is predicated on the primacy of the individual over the community, the haves over the have-nots, the living over the dead, and accumulation over participation and mutual responsibility.[40] The radical communal orientation of Día de los Muertos is a gift to the Church that corrects the creeping influence of consumerism and individualism. What the Church offers as a return gift is found in directing the energy and commitment for honoring the dead to the communion of Christ in the Eucharist.

When Ambrose led Monica to adapt the customs she had inherited from traditional African religions, he directed her to abandon the food and drink offerings that were part of the custom because those practices for the dead had become a mere occasion for revelry and intoxication. The issue was not the food and drink per se but what the food and drink were being used for: the indulgence of the living. The correction was for Monica to give the food to the hungry in honor of the dead, and to pour out her prayers for the dead to Christ in the Eucharist. Monica then offered the energy and investment of her devotions to the Lord, who pledges himself as the communion that the living and the dead seek.

The observance of Día de los Muertos is often met by Church authorities with varying levels of disapproval, mainly because the customs appear superstitious or incompatible with liturgical disciplines.[41] As with Ambrose and Monica, though, the issue ought not be the food, drink, and other tokens of ritual observance but what these things are ultimately used for. One traditional aspect of Día de los Muertos concerns welcoming the dead back into the households of the living; however, as we have seen throughout the past two chapters, the key in authentically Christian exercises of communion with the dead is the willingness of the living to go toward the dead in Christ rather than trying to pull the dead back to where we are. What, then, is the meaning of specific customs in Día de los Muertos?

Roberto Goizueta puts it like this:

> The function of home altars, food offerings to deceased relatives, visits to gravesites on Día de los Muertos . . . is precisely that of cementing bonds that link us to one another and that therefore define each of us as human persons. If a person is, at least in part, a physical, historical being, so too must the ties that bind us to one another be, at least in part, physical and historical.[42]

The physical, historical stuff between the living and the dead matters because the body matters. As we saw in our study of the creation of human beings and of resurrected, glorified bodies, God creates us in solidarity and raises us, in Christ, as whole and complete persons. To be a "person" means to be relational. The tokens that accompany Día de los Muertos are of course subject to commodification, consumerism, and mere spectacle—just like all religious devotions—but the central insight in gathering mementos of and even offerings for the dead is, as Goizueta points out, to make manifest the ties that bind us, which are stronger than death. This is a profoundly Christian insight that is proven true in Christ. This promise of Día de los Muertos is fulfilled when the longing and concern for the dead is directed, in the end, to the Eucharist.

Without learning from and following—even in adapted fashion—religious devotions like Día de los Muertos, we may well find ourselves bringing *too little* as an altar offering at the Liturgy of the Eucharist. As with Monica and Augustine after her, the duty of Christians who seek communion with the beloved dead is to bring our own sacrifices of prayer and charity to the altar and ask the Lord to give us the communion we cannot create ourselves. Then, upon receiving the gift of the Lord's communion in the sacrament, we have the duty and the privilege to live as though that communion truly is the rule of life.

If the ritual observances associated with suffering and death that are common to Mexican and other Latino cultures appear to some as merely the glorification of the macabre, then the fundamental insight and conviction behind these observances have likely been lost. These are celebrations not primarily of death but of the power of life that conquers death. That life comes by way of relationships, community, and mutual concern, and it vanquishes isolation, autonomy, and mere individual existence. The longing for and implicit belief in such life arose from the traditional religious customs where the beloved dead were not cast off to oblivion but held close to the living. In the person of Christ, that longing and belief receive a response in the Word made flesh.

To hold to Christ in the Sacrament of his Body and Blood but to fail to seek in him communion with the beloved dead would mean a failure to seek in him what he promises. When joined with liturgical observance, the revival of pious devotions that express and seek communion with the dead do not so much bring the dead back to earth as they raise the living toward the dead who rest in Christ. The Lord commands the living to seek their beloved dead in him as the real and specific persons whom we love, and even as the ones who, like John Cavadini's erstwhile classmate, have no one else to pray for them.

THE HEALING OF THE WHOLE: PURGATORY

The concern of the living for the dead mirrors the concern of the saints in heaven for us. Thérèse of Lisieux longed to spend her heaven doing good on earth.[43] Teresa of Calcutta wanted to give light to those in darkness on earth.[44] Origen taught that the joy of the saints will be complete only when no member of Christ's body is lacking. The saints are the ones who say to the living, "You are awaited."

Remembering the dead is how the living wait for the fullness of joy. John Cavadini waited on the bus for the unpopular boy at the end of the route, and now he prays for that man, that he may be surprised by love. Augustine learned how to offer his grief for lost friends, a lost son, and even his lost mother into a continuous prayer for their well-being in the Lord. Families who seek their beloved dead on Día de los Muertos reveal that they are not whole without those who have died. These are ways the living bear the pain of the dead with the dead, allowing their own joy to be bound up with the joy of those whom they love. Only together will Christ's joy be complete in us and for us.

Heaven is communion with Christ, in Christ. When Augustine prayed that his mother's sins be forgiven, he prayed that she be made fully capable of that communion. When John Cavadini prays for the man who died alone and who bore many wounds, including the wounds of others' hardness of heart, he prays that he may be made capable of Christ's communion. This inwardly necessary process of transformation, which also concerns the renewal and perfection of the human body to become capable of the full measure of love, is the heart of the Church's doctrine of purgatory. For sinners to become saints, the love of Christ must heal and change us. And since we are never ourselves by ourselves but always bound up in our relationships with others, the healing and sanctification of each person has social dimensions, for both the living and the dead.

Christ is the one who offers his life for the many. He gives himself so that others may live, and live in him. His life becomes our life. Ratzinger calls this "self-substituting love" and then goes on to explain the social dimensions of purgatory based upon that fundamental Christian truth: "Self-substituting love is a central Christian reality, and the doctrine of Purgatory states that for such love the limit of death does not exist. The possibility of helping and giving does not cease to exist on the death of the Christian. Rather does it stretch out to encompass the entire communion of saints, on both sides of death's portals."[45] When the saints concern themselves with the needs of sinners still on pilgrimage in this life or with the healing and strengthening of the souls in purgatory, they share in the "self-substituting love" of Christ. The saints' concern reveals their communion in Christ. When the living concern themselves with remaining in relationship with the dead and praying for the well-being of the dead, the living, though sinners still in need of the full measure of grace's healing themselves, already share in the life of the saints, for the Church's prayer over the offerings on the Solemnity of All Saints' is fulfilled in them: that "we may experience [the saints'] concern for our salvation." We experience that concern when we exercise that concern for others, whether living or dead. As the theologian Brett Salkeld powerfully claims, "Perhaps the most effective prayer we can make for our own beloved dead is to offer them forgiveness for the hurts they left behind in us."[46] Along with that forgiveness, we may also give thanks for the love they have given us.

The souls of our beloved dead are made perfect in Christ when the mercy that consumes the saints also consumes them. At the resurrection of the body, every part of who they are will radiate that mercy unto everlasting charity. And in the end, we who now long for our dead will discover in our own beloved dead the most beautiful surprise of all: they await us.

EPILOGUE: PASTORAL PRIORITIES AND CULTURAL RENEWAL

There is a solitary phone booth in a residential garden in Ōtsuchi, Japan. The garden is on a hill overlooking the Pacific—the same sea that rose up to engulf the land during the 2011 tsunami. Those waters separated loved ones from one another up and down the coast. Those who remained after the waters receded began to live with the pain of loss. In the years that followed, some of the survivors started to journey to the solitary phone booth on the hill, where they speak to dead loved ones through the disconnected phone.

The "Phone of the Wind" draws out the deepest desires of those who live on after their loved ones have died. They seek connection, they seek reunion, they seek communication. A telephone is an instrument that promises such things, but the gap the living wish to bridge is broader than any technological device can span. People know this phone is disconnected, they know they cannot reach their loved ones, and yet, strangely, they feel that they must try. People come to seek and speak, finding solace as they confront the undeniable separation. One man says to his daughter, "Show me where you are and I will build a house in the same place." Another says, "I feel like you are still alive somewhere."[1]

These Japanese pilgrims show others who mourn the paradoxical way forward: let your pain lead you. They are desperate to reach the ones they love. Their journey to the phone in the garden commits them to the importance of those who have died. In a world where the denial of death has become commonplace, they make their lonely pilgrimages to seek some kind of communion in death.

For Christians, the instrument of communication with the dead is Christ himself. To seek the dead in him requires an act of faith: trusting that Christ is who he has shown himself to be and that he gives what he promises. He does not cancel out the pain of loss; he offers himself as a way to make that loss meaningful. Those who seek in him will find. And yet the challenge is always the willingness to seek: to enter into grieving, to persist in longing, and to bring it all to him.

The Church bears the responsibility of seeking communion between the living and the dead. The Church indeed has a duty to proclaim this communion in doctrine, but that is not the Church's only duty. She must also and especially place pastoral priority on fostering the kind of cultures and propagating the kind of practices that form and empower the faithful to desire and act on this call to communion. As the old customs that once facilitated communion between the dead and living—and the healthy and the dying—have broken down, this pastoral priority has become more and more urgent. This is about the art of accompaniment, on both sides of the grave. In both places, "Jesus Christ is Lord" (Phil 2:11).

In the Church, there should be no lonely pilgrims seeking their beloved dead alone. There should be no forgotten dead. There should be no breaks in the bonds of communion. And there should be no lack of care for those outside the Church, who grieve and long for their beloved dead, too.

The pastoral creativity and personal investment necessary for renewing in the Church the cultures and customs for a living communion with the dead are immense. This is about more than perfecting funeral liturgies and eulogies, as important as that work may be. This is about developing the disciplined habits that make death familiar again, empower people to turn toward those who are suffering, include the dying in the life of society, and charge us all with the hard work of remembrance. In closing, I wish to suggest five practices for cultivating this culture of communion between the living and the dead.

1. THE REGULARITY OF PRAYER

Dorothy Day kept a list of the dead for whom she would pray. John Cavadini took on her practice. Quoting a seventeenth-century French Jesuit in a letter to a grieving mother, Fr. François René Blot recommends making such a practice regular while also suggesting that Christ, in his great mercy, allows our beloved dead to respond to our fidelity with their own charity:

> Make a list [of those you know who have died], and once a year, or rather once a week, read it over, and invoke those inscribed on it. This habit can only be productive of a more ardent desire to meet again, in heaven, the happy number of those who were united to you on earth. How great will be your bliss when

> you obtain from God, through their intercession,
> gifts that you have long solicited in vain. For I do
> not doubt that by their intervention our prayers are
> sometimes answered. If they loved us living, and
> could not find in their hearts to refuse our requests,
> how will it not be with them now, since their charity
> has become far more ardent and they are in so much
> greater favor with God.[2]

Just as the Church marks time by the feasts of saints and the mysteries of the life of Christ, so may the faithful mark the time of their own lives within the liturgical year by personal prayers and acts of remembrance for their own beloved dead. The key to Dorothy Day's discipline and the practice that Fr. Blot recommends is to make these observances regular.

Keep an actual list of the dead for whom you pray. Keep a book of the dead in your home. Include among the dead for whom you (and your family) pray not just those who were dear to you in life but also those who may not have been dear to you, even those more your enemies than your friends. Include also those who would have no one else to pray for them, like the boy who sat next to John Cavadini on the bus. Offer prayers for your dead weekly, perhaps all at once or divvied up among different days of the week. Be especially attentive to the anniversaries of death, and be sure to ask for a Mass to be offered for them on those days.

My own children, especially my youngest children, regularly pray for "Grandpa Joe and Grandma Shirley" during our own family's night prayer. These were our next-door neighbors, who died a few years ago, both in their nineties. Without these nightly prayers, our children would, in time, likely forget these two beautiful people who loved them so well. By recalling them in prayer, our kids keep these beloved dead a part of their lives, seeking communion with them.

2. THE HARD WORK OF MEMORY

For the 2020 Super Bowl, Google ran an ad called "Loretta."[3] The voice of an elderly man opens the ad saying, "Hey Google, show me photos of me and Loretta." You then see a series of photos, spanning different decades, of this man with his now deceased wife, Loretta. He laughs and reminisces as the photos show on the screen. He tells Google to make notes for him about the photos and his own memories. It is a moving commercial that I have shown in a course I teach to undergraduate students. I ask the students, "What's missing?" Invariably, they say, "Other people." No family is involved. The whole premise of the ad is that Google can remember for you. This is not what we need.

A friend of mine recently told me what his grandmother does for his family. Her husband—my friend's grandfather—died years ago. Every month, she writes a letter to the family telling them something about their grandfather or passing on a story from their family's life. Every year, there are twelve letters. When the family gets together for reunions, they spend some time talking about the stories and the memories. The grandmother is the bearer of memory for her family, and her family makes the memories their own. The memories are the responsibility of the family, and they all engage in the hard but delightful work of passing on those memories. This seems to me an important counter-practice to our over-Googled lives.

Oral and written testimony of our loved ones and of family histories is a practice to reclaim. It is *always* easier to outsource memory: to snap a photo, to leave a voice memo, and then move along. But then the memories exist *outside* of you. It is actually a way of being unburdened, and being unburdened is the opposite of love. The work of memory is essential to honoring the dead. In family homes and in parishes, we should become more practiced in telling the stories of our loved ones.

3. THE RETURN OF MOURNING

In her memoir concerning the death of her mother, Megan O'Rourke speaks of a peculiar kind of envy: "After my mother's death, I felt the lack of rituals to shape and support my loss. I found myself envying my Jewish friends the practice of saying Kaddish, with its ceremonious designation of time each day devoted to remembering the lost person. As I drifted through the hours, I wondered: What does it mean to grieve when we have so few rituals for observing and externalizing loss?"[4] What O'Rourke feels is the loss of what was once customary: the year of mourning or some version of it. As Thomas Lynch notes, this period of public mourning "granted to the bereaved some time to grieve as well as outlining customs meant to assist the mourner."[5]

If what Philippe Ariès says about the "modern approach" to death is true, then the general taboo against public mourning is an indignity visited upon those who grieve. It is also a telltale sign of how we have moved death and the processes of dying away from communal life and into private corners where individuals bear the weight alone. The remedy—and thus the pastoral priority—is to redevelop prescribed, ritualized, and routine practices for mourning that unfold over a notable period of time. This is a gift to mourners, as it relieves them of the burden of having to figure out what to do with their grief on their own, like the young Augustine collapsing into his "black grief." It is also a debt of honor paid to the dead, who are thereby permitted to interrupt the otherwise "normal" happenings of the fast-paced world. As is so often the case, haste is the enemy of humanity. Mourning slows us down.

This priority goes hand in hand with actively accompanying the dying and committing the community to the suffering of the sick. In the modern world, we are blessed with extraordinary means for health care and medical treatments, but when these means are used as a substitute for communal care, our practices become less than fully human. Both the acceptance of mourning and the accompaniment of the sick and dying require changes to "normal" life. Those changes will make us more rather than less human.

4. RELIQUARIES OF THE ORDINARY

The first time I talked with Stephanie DePrez (chapter 1) about the death of her mother and her own mourning, she told me that she happened to be wearing her mother's earrings and one of her rings. In reference to these tokens she said, "The relics of my mother's life I treat as holy." In other words, she cherishes the physical things that connect her to her mother, and (through her own theological musings) she has determined that if she hopes for her mother's glorious resurrection, she should treat the earthly things she left behind as relics of a saint.

Stephanie is not presuming to canonize her mother by her own power. Rather, she is allowing her hope for her mother to change how she, Stephanie, regards things in the created world *now*.

As someone who is overly slow to get rid of things, I recognize the potential downside here: we become hoarders who overvalue even the minutest minutiae. On the other side, though, we find the promptings of ease, where it is always easier to move on than it is to hold to. The pastoral practice here therefore seems to be in finding ways to properly honor the "stuff" of people's lives and especially those "relics" that connect us to our beloved dead.

This is the way of honoring and continuing to cherish their *bodily* presence, which is the same body that, in the fullness of time, will be raised in glory, God willing.

5. PUBLIC WORKS OF COMMUNION

The "holiday shopping season" starts earlier every year. It is a public period of preparation for what has been deemed an important societal event: ostensibly Christmas, but more the commercialization of Christmas. My point here, though, is that the intense and increasingly prolonged period of preparation testifies to what has been communally agreed upon as important.

If we return to the observance of Día de los Muertos, especially in places like Oaxaca, Mexico, or even certain neighborhoods in the United States, we see something similar. The intensity of the preparation and prolonged period of planning testify to the importance of what is being observed. In this case, it is relationship with the dead that is being prized.

I love All Saints' Day, and All Souls' Day right along with it. But if these come and go once a year with very little before or after being affected, then what the Church celebrates on days like these has not been lifted up as sufficiently important, at least not in practice. If Masses offered throughout the year for the dead are not accompanied by almsgiving or other acts of charity, then something has been lost. In seeking communion with the dead, the Church has the responsibility and the opportunity to be a light to others. This light must shine from parishes and families in the midst of concrete communities, with the fervor for charity common to the saints.

The point of making the works of communion public is not to create a spectacle but rather to provide a witness and a source of hope and healing. Public Eucharistic processions in honor of the saints, or the victims of gun violence or abortion, or those who have no one else to pray for them change the way the space of a community appears. Here, in the midst of humdrum life, people commit their bodies and their prayers to remembering and honoring those who are otherwise unseen and unheard. Monthly adoration devoted to prayers for the souls in purgatory changes the way a parish community thinks about its own prayer life and its parish boundaries. An ongoing ministry of a large number of parishioners to accompany grieving families in both the short and long term changes the basic assumption about who bears the pain of loss.

The pain of loss points us toward the hard work of seeking communion. The more that pain is shared, the more it takes on the dimensions of Christ's love. Communion with the dead comes from the communion of Christ when the living allow that communion to transform their lives.

NOTES

INTRODUCTION

1. Portions of the story I have written about Louis and Dorothy DeLorenzo first appeared in *America Magazine*. See Leonard DeLorenzo, "The Journey from All Saints to All Souls," *America Magazine*, November 2, 2015, http://americamagazine.org/issue/holy-ones-loved-ones.

2. "Paradise Polled: Americans and the Afterlife," Roper Center for Public Opinion Research, accessed June 11, 2021, https://ropercenter.cornell.edu/paradise-polled-americans-and-afterlife.

3. The Jesuit theologian Karl Rahner speaks to this hole in the average Christian's religious imagination in "Why and How Can We Venerate the Saints?," in *Theological Investigations*, trans. Cornelius Ernst et al. (Limerick, Ireland: Mary Immaculate College, 2000), 8:6–7.

4. Karl Rahner has another essay that relates to this point: "The Eternal Significance of the Humanity of Jesus for Our Relationship with God," in *Theological Investigations*, 3:35–46.

5. Barna Group, "Americans Describe Their Views about Life after Death," Research, Culture & Media, Barna, October 21, 2003, https://www.barna.com/research/americans-describe-their-views-about-life-after-death/.

6. When asked about belief in bodily resurrection, only 37 percent of all Americans in the last decade claimed this belief, including only about half of the Catholic population. See Andrew Litschi et

al., *Relationships in America Survey* (Austin, TX: Austin Institute for the Study of Family and Culture, 2014).

7. In 2016, Gallup found that 71 percent of Americans believed in life after death, against 17 percent who did not, with the remainder unsure (see "Paradise Polled"). These results are mirrored in the 2014 *Relationships in America Survey*, which found that 72 percent of Americans believed in life after death, including nearly 80 percent of Catholics (Litschi et al., *Relationships in America Survey*).

8. See John Henry Newman, *An Essay in Aid of a Grammar of Assent* (Notre Dame, IN: University of Notre Dame Press, 1979), 93; and Timothy P. O'Malley, *Real Presence: What Does It Mean and Why Does It Matter?* (Notre Dame, IN: Ave Maria Press, 2021), 9–10.

1. THE SEPARATION OF DEATH AND THE COMMUNION OF CHRIST

1. Leonard J. DeLorenzo, "Life Is Changed but Something Ended, with Stephanie DePrez," in *Church Life Today*, July 19, 2021, podcast, 42:26, https://bit.ly/life-is-changed-something-ended.

2. Irenaeus of Lyons, *Against Heresies*, ed. Alexander Roberts, James Donaldson, and Arthur Cleveland Coxe (Ex Fontibus Company, 2012), 345 [III.6.5].

3. Irenaeus, *Against Heresies*, 361 [III.18.7].

4. Irenaeus, *Against Heresies*, 361 [III.18.7].

5. This section draws, in part, from my *Turn to the Lord: Forming Disciples for Lifelong Conversion* (Collegeville, MN: Liturgical Press, 2021), 68–70; also present in the same page range of Leonard J. DeLorenzo, *Turn to the Lord: An Invitation to Lifelong Conversion* (Collegeville, MN: Liturgical Press, 2021).

6. See N. T. Wright, *Christian Origins and the Question of God*, vol. 3, *The Resurrection of the Son of God* (Minneapolis: Fortress Press, 2003), 733.

7. Hans Urs von Balthasar, *Theo-Drama: Theological Dramatic Theory, vol 5, The Last Act*, trans. Graham Harrison (San Francisco: Ignatius Press, 1998), 222.

8. Joseph Ratzinger captures this whole mystery in one sweep: "Christ does not die in the noble detachment of the philosopher. He dies in tears. On his lips was the bitter taste of abandonment and isolation in all its horror. Here the hubris that would be the equal of God is contrasted with an acceptance of the cup of being human, down to its last dregs." Joseph Ratzinger, *Eschatology: Death and Eternal Life*, ed. Aidan Nichols, trans. Michael Waldstein, 2nd ed. (Washington, DC: Catholic University of America Press, 2007), 102.

9. "From an Ancient Homily for Holy Saturday: The Lord's Descent into Hell," accessed June 16, 2021, https://www.vatican.va/spirit/documents/spirit_20010414_omelia-sabato-santo_en.html.

10. "Lord's Descent into Hell."

11. "Lord's Descent into Hell."

12. "Lord's Descent into Hell."

13. "Lord's Descent into Hell."

14. Joseph Ratzinger expresses this mystery succinctly: "In the descent of Jesus, God himself descends into Sheol. At that moment, death ceases to be the God-forsaken land of darkness, a realm of unpitying distance from God. In Christ, God himself entered that realm of death, transforming the space of noncommunication into the place of his own presence." Ratzinger, *Eschatology*, 93. We might compare this to Hans Urs von Balthasar's biblically constructed comment on the descent of Christ into solitariness in *Mysterium*

Paschale: The Mystery of Easter, trans. Aidan Nichols (San Francisco: Ignatius Press, 2000), 162–63; Hans Urs von Balthasar, *Theo-Drama: Theological Dramatic Theory*, vol. 3, *The Dramatis Personae: The Person in Christ*, trans. Graham Harrison (San Francisco: Ignatius Press, 1993), 245–50; and Leonard J. DeLorenzo, *Work of Love: A Theological Reconstruction of the Communion of Saints* (Notre Dame, IN: University of Notre Dame Press, 2017), 74–95.

15. Irenaeus, *Against Heresies*, 570 [V.7.2].

16. Irenaeus, *Against Heresies*, 361 [III.18.7].

17. For more on this necessary transformation, especially in regard to the Easter encounters with the risen Christ, see Wright, *Resurrection of the Son*, 659–61; Rowan Williams, *Resurrection: Interpreting the Easter Gospel* (New York: Pilgrim Press, 1984), 44–45; and DeLorenzo, *Work of Love*, 107–15.

2. HEAVEN AND THE HORIZON OF HOPE

1. Laura Kelly Fanucci, "This Is the Story I Have to Tell You," *Mothering Spirit* (blog), March 3, 2016, https://motheringspirit.com/2016/03/this-is-the-story-i-have-to-tell-you/.

2. Fanucci, "This Is the Story."

3. Fanucci, "This Is the Story."

4. Laura Kelly Fanucci talked about this experience along with her understanding of heaven and eternal life on Leonard J. DeLorenzo, "Heaven in the Midst of Death, with Laura Kelly Fanucci," in *Church Life Today*, July 19, 2021, podcast, 36:09, https://bit.ly/heaven-in-death.

5. Fanucci, "This Is the Story."

6. I address this issue of imagining heaven according to a kind of destination obsession in Leonard J. DeLorenzo, "Hide and Seek: The Eschatology of *Introduction to Christianity*," in *Gift to the Church and*

World: Fifty Years of Joseph Ratzinger's Introduction to Christianity, ed. John C. Cavadini and Donald Wallenfang (Eugene, OR: Pickwick, 2021), 241–54.

7. Joseph Ratzinger, *Eschatology: Death and Eternal Life*, ed. Aidan Nichols, trans. Michael Waldstein, 2nd ed. (Washington, DC: Catholic University of America Press, 2007), 8.

8. Fanucci, "This Is the Story."

9. Irenaeus of Lyons, *Against Heresies*, ed. Alexander Roberts, James Donaldson, and Arthur Cleveland Coxe (Ex Fontibus, 2012), 332–35 [III.XIX]; see also Gregory of Nanzianzus, *Orationes* 1, 5: SC 247, 78, quoted in Benedict XVI, "General Audience of 22 August 2007: Saint Gregory Nazianzus (2)," http://www.vatican.va/content/benedict-xvi/en/audiences/2007/documents/hf_ben-xvi_aud_20070822.html.

10. For an account of how Christ accomplishes our union with his Father through prayer, see Leonard J. DeLorenzo, *Into the Heart of the Father: Learning from and Giving Yourself through Christ in Prayer* (Frederick, MD: Word Among Us, 2021).

11. Augustine, *The Trinity*, ed. John Rotelle, trans. Edmund Hill (Hyde Park, NY: New City Press, 2012), I.18. While meditating on another of Christ's mysteries—the finding of Jesus in the Temple at age twelve—Balthasar offers an illuminating comment that resonates with Augustine's: "We find him definitively only in the place of the Father, in heaven, which is to say when finding no longer implies containing God within our space, but rather when it means that we have been found by God, that we have entered into his space, then we are 'known by God' (1 Cor 13:12)." (Hans Urs von Balthasar, *The Threefold Garland: The World's Salvation in Mary's Prayer* (San Francisco: Ignatius Press, 1982), 60. For a splendid commentary on Augustine's understanding of the movement from seeing what

is below to seeing what is above in Christ, see Khaled Anatolios, *Retrieving Nicaea: The Development and Meaning of Trinitarian Doctrine* (Grand Rapids, MI: Baker Academic, 2011), 248.

12. Jean Corbon, *The Wellspring of Worship*, trans. Matthew O'Connell, 2nd ed. (San Francisco: Ignatius Press, 2005), 61–62. The previous paragraph draws from my book, *Into the Heart of the Father*, 59–60.

13. Thomas Aquinas, *Summa Theologiae* (New Advent), Suppl., q.82, a.1, co, https://www.newadvent.org/summa/5082.htm.

14. Thomas Aquinas, *Of God and His Creatures: An Annotated Translation of "The Summa contra Gentiles" of Saint Thomas Aquinas*, trans. Joseph Rickaby (Whitefish, MT: Kessinger, 2010), IV.86.3.

15. Aquinas, *Summa contra Gentiles*, IV.86.4; cf. Aquinas, ST, Suppl., q.83, a.1.

16. Aquinas, *Summa contra Gentiles*, IV.86.2; cf. Aquinas, ST, Suppl., q.84, a.1.

17. Paul Claudel, *I Believe in God: A Meditation on the Apostles' Creed* (New York: Holt, Rinehart and Winston, 1963), 279–80.

18. David Foster Wallace, "Roger Federer as Religious Experience," *New York Times*, August 20, 2006, https://www.nytimes.com/2006/08/20/sports/playmagazine/20federer.html.

19. G. K. Chesterton offers a memorable account of the vitality of children in relation to God in *Orthodoxy* (San Francisco: Ignatius Press, 1995), 65–66; as does Charles Péguy all throughout *The Portal of the Mystery of Hope*, trans. David Louis Schindler Jr. (Grand Rapids, MI: William B. Eerdmans, 1996).

20. Aquinas, *Summa contra Gentiles*, IV.86.1; cf. Aquinas, ST, Suppl., q.85, a.1.

21. Irenaeus, *Against Heresies*, 461 [IV.20.7].

22. Claudel, *I Believe in God*, 281.

23. Laura Kelly Fanucci, "The Dark Side of Light," *Mothering Spirit* (blog), April 7, 2016, https://motheringspirit.com/2016/04/the-dark-side-of-light/.

24. Quoted in Edward Kim, "Heaven Is a World of Love by Jonathan Edwards," *The Doctrine of Election Is the Sum of the Gospel* (blog), March 27, 2002, https://edwardkim.wordpress.com/2002/03/27/heaven-is-a-world-of-love-by-jonathan-edwards/.

25. Jonathan Edwards, "Heaven Is a World of Love," sermon 15 [1749], in *Ethical Writings (Works of Jonathan Edwards Online Volume 8)*, ed. Paul Ramsey (New Haven, CT: Jonathan Edwards Center at Yale University, 1989), 370, including endnote 1, http://edwards.yale.edu/archive?path=aHR0cDovL2Vkd2FyZHMueWFsZS-5lZHUvY2dpLWJpbi9uZXdwaGlsby9nZXRvYmplY3QucGw/Yy43OjQ6MTUud2plbw==.

26. Edwards, "Heaven Is a World," 374–75.

27. Edwards, "Heaven Is a World," 379.

28. Cf. Irenaeus, *Against Heresies*, 453 [IV.18.5].

3. LOSS AND THE LONGING FOR WHOLENESS

1. Robert Cording, "In the Unwalled City," *Image Journal*, no. 109 (2021), https://imagejournal.org/article/in-the-unwalled-city/.

2. Leonard J. DeLorenzo, "Life in Death in Life, with Robert Cording," in *Church Life Today*, August 2, 2021, podcast, 30:27, https://bit.ly/life-in-death.

3. Cording, "In the Unwalled City."

4. Quoted in Henri de Lubac, *Catholicism: Christ and the Common Destiny of Man*, trans. Lancelot Sheppard and Elizabeth Englund (San Francisco: Ignatius Press, 1988), 13.

5. For more on this theological notion of personhood, see Joseph Ratzinger, "Concerning the Notion of Person in Theology," *Communio* 17 (Fall 1990): 438–54.

6. For more on the meaning of Christ's body, see Karl Rahner, "The Eternal Significance of the Humanity of Jesus for Our Relationship with God," in *Theological Investigations*, trans. Cornelius Ernst et al. (Limerick, Ireland: Mary Immaculate College, 2000), 3:35–46.

7. This reflection on the meaning of the body is a commentary on Irenaeus of Lyons, *Against Heresies*, ed. Alexander Roberts, James Donaldson, and Arthur Cleveland Coxe (Ex Fontibus, 2012), 570 [V.7.2].

8. Quoted in Joseph Ratzinger, *Eschatology: Death and Eternal Life*, ed. Aidan Nichols, trans. Michael Waldstein, 2nd ed. (Washington, DC: Catholic University of America Press, 2007), 185; see also Leonard J. DeLorenzo, *Work of Love: A Theological Reconstruction of the Communion of Saints* (Notre Dame, IN: University of Notre Dame Press, 2017), 221–23.

9. Quoted in Ratzinger, *Eschatology*, 186; cf. de Lubac, *Catholicism*, 126.

10. Ratzinger, *Eschatology*, 187.

11. Ratzinger, *Eschatology*, 188.

12. For more on the desire for the good of another as the inner dynamism of love, consider St. Thomas Aquinas on the questions of "Is union an effect of love?" and "Is mutual indwelling an effect of love?" in *Summa Theologiae* (New Advent), I-II, q.28, a.1–2, https://www.newadvent.org/summa/5082.htm.

13. Thérèse of Lisieux, *St. Thérèse of Lisieux: Her Last Conversations*, trans. John Clarke (Washington, DC: Institute of Carmelite Studies Publications, 1977), 102.

14. Teresa of Calcutta, *Come Be My Light: The Private Writings of the "Saint of Calcutta,"* ed. Brian Kolodiejchuk (New York: Doubleday, 2007), 230.

15. Teresa of Calcutta, *Come Be My Light*, 232.

16. Ratzinger, *Eschatology*, 188.

17. Appealing in part to Jacques Maritain, Philippe Ariès claims that this cultural attitude emerged in the United States and was then exported to the old continent. See, for example, Philippe Ariès, *Western Attitudes toward Death: From the Middle Ages to the Present*, trans. Patricia Ranum (Baltimore: Johns Hopkins University Press, 1975), 94.

18. Ratzinger, *Eschatology*, 69–70.

19. Ratzinger, *Eschatology*, 72; see also Jurgen Moltmann, *The Coming of God: Christian Eschatology*, trans. Margaret Kohl (Minneapolis: Fortress Press, 2004), 50–57; and especially Romano Guardini, *The End of the Modern World*, trans. Elinor Briefs (Wilmington, DE: ISI Books, 1998), 111, which is an endnote to page 97.

20. Ratzinger, *Eschatology*, 69–70.

21. Philippe Ariès, *The Hour of Our Death: The Classic History of Western Attitudes toward Death over the Last One Thousand Years*, trans. Helen Weaver, 2nd ed. (New York: Vintage Books, 2008), 22; cf. Ariès, *Western Attitudes toward Death*, 7–25.

22. Ariès, *Western Attitudes toward Death*, 51–52; see also 37.

23. Ariès, *Western Attitudes toward Death*, 59; see also 70.

24. Ariès, *Hour of Our Death*, 300.

25. Ariès, *Hour of Our Death*, 560.

26. Ariès, *Hour of Our Death*, 587.

27. Ariès, *Hour of Our Death*, 583; cf. Geoffrey Gorer, "The Pornography of Death," in *Death, Grief, and Mourning* (New York: Arno Press, 1977), 199.

28. On the inhumanity of not facing grief and engaging in mourning, see Thomas Long and Thomas Lynch, *The Good Funeral: Death, Grief, and the Community of Care* (Louisville, KY: Westminster John Knox Press, 2013), especially 231.

29. Ariès, *Western Attitudes toward Death*, 88–89. Lawrence Samuel speaks of the connection between the modern conception of the "self" and the professionalization of dying and death in his *Death, American Style: A Cultural History of Dying in America* (New York: Rowman & Littlefield, 2013), especially 124.

30. Ariès, *Hour of Our Death*, 94.

31. Ernest Becker argues toward the same end in *The Denial of Death* (New York: Free Press, 1975).

32. Ariès, *Hour of Our Death*, 613.

33. Long and Lynch, *Good Funeral*, 60; see also 184–86.

34. The "modern approach" is not universal in the "modern world," even in the Western Hemisphere. In places like the Mexican town of Oaxaca with strong customs of remembrance, the attitudes toward death and dying match up nearly perfectly with the "classic approach" Ariès describes. See Shawn D. Haley and Curt Fukuda, *Day of the Dead: When Two Worlds Meet in Oaxaca* (New York: Berghahn, 2004), 27.

35. Ariès, *Hour of Our Death*, 613. The preceding section draws, in part, from my *Work of Love*, especially 26–31.

36. Cording, "In the Unwalled City."

37. Dietrich Bonhoeffer, *Letters and Papers from Prison*, ed. Eberhard Bethge (Princeton, NJ: Touchstone, 1997), 176–77.

4. SACRED MEMORY AND THE WORK OF MERCY

1. Leonard J. DeLorenzo, "Praying for the Dead, with John Cavadini," in *Church Life Today*, November 14, 2021, podcast, 31:39, https://bit.ly/praying-for-the-dead.

2. This practice of making a list of the dead for whom you regularly pray is recommended over and over again in Fr. François René Blot's beautiful letters to a grieving mother. See François René Blot, *In Heaven We'll Meet Again* (Manchester, NH: Sophia Institute, 2016), especially 94.

3. DeLorenzo, "Praying for the Dead, with John Cavadini."

4. Augustine, *The Confessions*, trans. Maria Boulding (New York: Vintage Books, 1998), 58 [IV.4.7].

5. Augustine, *Confessions*, 59 [IV.8].

6. Augustine, *Confessions*, 59 [IV.9].

7. Augustine, *Confessions*, 59 [IV.9].

8. Augustine, *Confessions*, 174 [IX.6].

9. Augustine, *Confessions*, 180 [IX.6.14].

10. Augustine, *Confessions*, 180 [IX.6.14].

11. Augustine, *Confessions*, 180 [IX.6.14].

12. Augustine, *Confessions*, 193 [IX.31].

13. Augustine, *Confessions*, 193 [IX.32].

14. Augustine, *Confessions*, 194 [IX.13.34].

15. Augustine, *Confessions*, 195 [IX.13.34].

16. Augustine, *Confessions*, 195 [IX.36], cf. 190 [11.27].

17. Augustine, *Confessions*, 196 [IX.37].

18. Michael Driscoll and J. Michael Joncas, *The Order of Mass: A Roman Missal Study Edition and Workbook* (Collegeville, MN: Liturgical Press, 2011), 89–90.

19. Driscoll and Joncas, *Order of Mass*, 86.

20. Driscoll and Joncas, *Order of Mass*, 96.

21. Driscoll and Joncas, *Order of Mass*, 85.

22. Driscoll and Joncas, *Order of Mass*, 96.

23. Driscoll and Joncas, *Order of Mass*, 95.

24. For more on this movement from and toward Christ in the Eucharist, see Jean-Luc Marion, *The Idol and Distance: Five Studies*, trans. Thomas A. Carlson, 2nd ed. (New York: Fordham University Press, 2001), especially 118, 129, and 132; Louis-Marie Chauvet, "The Broken Bread as Theological Figure of Eucharistic Presence," in *Sacramental Presence in a Postmodern Context*, ed. L. Boeve and L. Leijssen (Leuven: Leuven University Press, 2001), 260–61; and Kimberly Belcher, *Efficacious Engagement: Sacramental Participation in the Trinitarian Mystery* (Collegeville, MN: Liturgical Press, 2011), 32–46.

25. Daughters of Saint Paul, ed., *Saint Paul Daily Missal* (Boston: Pauline Books & Media, 2012), 2344.

26. Daughters of Saint Paul, ed., *Saint Paul Daily Missal*, 2349.

27. Daughters of Saint Paul, ed., *Saint Paul Daily Missal*, 2559.

28. For more on the art of dying as an act of trust in God's care, see Romano Guardini, *Sacred Signs*, trans. Grace Branham (London: Aeterna Press, 2015), 34; and Romano Guardini, *Meditations before Mass*, trans. Elinor Briefs (Notre Dame, IN: Ave Maria Press, 2014), 95.

29. Daughters of Saint Paul, *Saint Paul Daily Missal*, 2566.

30. The preceding section on the prayers over the offerings draws significantly from my *Work of Love: A Theological Reconstruction of the Communion of Saints* (Notre Dame, IN: University of Notre Dame Press, 2017), 225–28; as well as my "The Journey from All Saints to All Souls," *America Magazine*, November 2, 2015, http://americamagazine.org/issue/holy-ones-loved-ones.

31. Augustine, *Confessions*, 98 [VI.2.2].

32. Roberto S. Goizueta, "The Symbolic World of Mexican American Religion," in *Horizons of the Sacred: Mexican Traditions in U.S. Catholicism*, ed. Timothy Matovina and Gary Riebe-Estrella (Ithaca, NY: Cornell University Press, 2002), 121.

33. Goizueta, "Symbolic World," 131.

34. Goizueta, "Symbolic World," 131.

35. Lara Medina and Gilbert R. Cadena, "Días de Los Muertos: Public Ritual, Community Renewal, and Popular Religion in Los Angeles," in *Horizons of the Sacred*, 75.

36. Medina and Cadena, "Días de Los Muertos," 75.

37. See Shawn D. Haley and Curt Fukuda, *Day of the Dead: When Two Worlds Meet in Oaxaca* (New York: Berghahn, 2004), 27, 136–38.

38. See again Philippe Ariès, *The Hour of Our Death: The Classic History of Western Attitudes toward Death over the Last One Thousand Years*, trans. Helen Weaver, 2nd ed. (New York: Vintage Books, 2008), 613.

39. Joseph Ratzinger, *Eschatology: Death and Eternal Life*, ed. Aidan Nichols, trans. Michael Waldstein, 2nd ed. (Washington, DC: Catholic University of America Press, 2007), 72.

40. Laura Pérez, "Spirit Glyphs: Reimagining Art and Artist in the Work of Chicana Tlamatinime," *Modern Fiction Studies* 44, no. 2 (Spring 1998): 43; cf. Medina and Cadena, "Días de Los Muertos," 86–88.

41. Timothy Matovina and Gary Riebe-Estrella, "Introduction," in *Horizons of the Sacred*, 1–7.

42. Goizueta, "Symbolic World," 123.

43. Thérèse of Lisieux, *St. Thérèse of Lisieux: Her Last Conversations*, trans. John Clarke (Washington, DC: Institute of Carmelite Studies Publications, 1977), 102.

44. Teresa of Calcutta, *Come Be My Light: The Private Writings of the "Saint of Calcutta,"* ed. Brian Kolodiejchuk (New York: Doubleday, 2007), 230.

45. Ratzinger, *Eschatology*, 232–33.

46. Brett Salkeld, "Guilt, Responsibility, and Purgatory: How Traditional Catholic Teaching Can Help Us Think about Truth, Reconciliation, and Reparations," *Church Life Journal*, September 30, 2021, https://churchlifejournal.nd.edu/articles/guilt-responsibility-and-purgatory-how-traditional-catholic-teaching-can-help-us-think-about-truth-reconciliation-and-reparations/.

EPILOGUE

1. *The Phone of the Wind: Whispers to Lost Families*, directed by Tomohiko Yokoyama and Ryo Urabe (Tokyo, Japan: NHK World, 2016), 49 min. See also Issei Kato and Mari Saito, "Japan's Tsunami Survivors Call Lost Loves on the Phone of the Wind," *The Wider Image*, April 7, 2021, https://widerimage.reuters.com/story/japans-tsunami-survivors-call-lost-loves-on-the-phone-of-the-wind.

2. Quoting Paul de Barry in François René Blot, *In Heaven We'll Meet Again* (Manchester, NH: Sophia Institute, 2016), 121.

3. Google, "Loretta," 2020, https://www.youtube.com/watch?v=PW6SocCjTMM.

4. Megan O'Rourke, *The Long Goodbye: A Memoir of Grief* (New York: Riverhead, 2011), 13; quoted in Thomas Long and Thomas Lynch, *The Good Funeral: Death, Grief, and the Community of Care* (Louisville, KY: Westminster John Knox Press, 2013), 62–63.

5. Long and Lynch, *Good Funeral*, 63.

Leonard J. DeLorenzo, PhD has worked at the McGrath Institute for Church Life since 2003 and teaches theology at the University of Notre Dame. He is an award-winning author who has written or edited eleven books, including *Witness* and *What Matters Most.*

Through the McGrath Institute, DeLorenzo is developing the Sullivan Family Saints Initiative, devoted to fostering scholarship on and devotion to the saints. He also launched, produces, and hosts *Church Life Today*—a popular radio show and podcast. In addition to writing books, articles, and essays, he speaks regularly in academic and pastoral settings on the saints, biblical catechesis, vocation and discernment, and the theological imagination, among other topics.

DeLorenzo and his wife, Lisa, live in South Bend, Indiana, with their children.

Website: leonardjdelorenzo.com
Newsletter: bit.ly/lifesweetnesshope
Twitter: @leodelo2
LinkedIn: https://www.linkedin.com/in/leonardjdelorenzo/

The McGrath Institute for Church Life was founded as the Center for Pastoral and Social Ministry by the late Notre Dame President Fr. Theodore Hesburgh, CSC, in 1976. The McGrath Institute partners with Catholic dioceses, parishes, and schools to provide theological education and formation to address pressing pastoral problems. The Institute connects the Catholic intellectual life to the life of the Church to form faithful Catholic leaders for service to the Church and the world. The McGrath Institute strives to be the preeminent source of creative Catholic content and programming for the new evangelization.

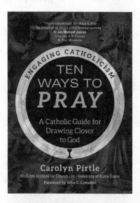

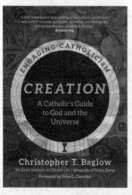
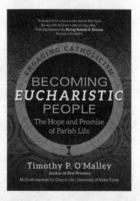